Equity Crowdfunding Explained

By Salvador Briggman

Introduction

When Facebook went public on the Nasdaq in 2012, many of Facebook's 3,000 employees became millionaires, and many more were handsomely rewarded for their dedication, commitment, and appetite for risk.

The same is true of countless IPOs throughout history from Google to Microsoft. The investors, employees, and partners that "got in early" reached a height of financial abundance that many ordinary folk only dream of.

Until recently, these types of startup investments were **only** accessible by the ultra-wealthy. They were **hidden** from ordinary investors, like you and me. Put simply, the government prohibited you from investing in early-stage startup companies. You couldn't just log onto an online marketplace and buy shares in the next hot startup, that is, until everyone already knew about it.

For a while, investors found these traditional regulations to be satisfactory. It helped protect them from risky companies with experimental prototypes. But, as time went on, that assent turned into outrage. The world watched as companies, like Oculus, created the next generation of virtual reality technology and then got acquired by Facebook for $3 billion dollars.

It might sound like a big win, but in reality, **none** of the 9,522 backers that pledged a total of $2.4 million to the Oculus Kickstarter campaign actually had any equity stake from the transaction. They were **pledging or donating** money, not investing it. They didn't really get a piece of the action.

There's no doubt that the world that we live in has been transformed by companies like Facebook, Uber, Tesla, Google, Amazon, and many more. Now, for the first time in history, you can not only be a part of that change, but you can also **profit** from it. You can become the next stakeholder in a fast-growing startup company that's on the path for an IPO or major acquisition.

This book is your passport into the new world of equity crowdfunding, where startups are raising money online from investors all over the world. You'll quickly learn about all the major platforms, what goes into an offering, tips for investors, and finally, you'll get a simple easy-to-understand breakdown of all of those confusing regulations.

My name is Salvador Briggman and I've been writing about crowdfunding since 2012 on my blog, CrowdCrux.com. I also host a podcast called Crowdfunding Demystified and have a YouTube channel on the same topic. I hope you enjoy this book, and if you do, take a sec to leave a review on Amazon!

- Sal

P.S. You can get access to a FREE video on equity crowdfunding regulations here: http://www.crowdcrux.com/equitybonus

"The effect you have on others is the most valuable currency there is." - Jim Carrey

Table of Contents

Chapter 1: What is Equity Crowdfunding?

The crowdfunding platform Kickstarter has taken the world by storm, having raised more than $3 billion for entrepreneurial and creative projects. While this is extremely impressive, Kickstarter is limited in one key way.

You can't actually own equity in the companies that you support. You can only pre-order the products that they create.

This has all changed!

As of May 2016, retail investors can now gain access to previously closed off deals via Title III of the Jobs act. This is also known as regulation CF or regulation crowdfunding.

Equity crowdfunding platforms have emerged to connect startups with investors looking to get on the ground floor of new companies that have the potential to be the next Uber, Facebook, or Google.

Despite this first step towards the democratization of funding, there is still a lot of confusion around how equity crowdfunding works and how you can use it. In this chapter, I'm going to cover all of this, along with explaining the different types of equity crowdfunding.

I'll be giving you an overview of what equity crowdfunding is, how you can use it, and some of the high-level benefits and drawbacks of this new financial tool. We'll be going more in-depth into the legal implications in Chapter 2.

How can YOU use equity crowdfunding?

You can use "equity crowdfunding" to raise money online for a startup company from a pool of investors, referred to as "the crowd."

Each equity crowdfunding campaign has:

- A fundraising goal
- Funding duration
- Deal terms
- A pitch that investors will use to learn more about the startup

The pitch contains a pitch video, attractive images, and campaign text that describes the company and offering. After looking through the pitch video and the campaign text, an investor can then decide whether or not they'd like to own a bit of the company. There may be an investment minimum, which varies from deal to deal.

As long as the deal is still open, you'll be able to invest in the company and own equity in the startup. Pretty cool, huh?

Previously, a founder might raise money initially from a small group of angel investors. In later stages, they might bring in more angels or a VC firm. Under new this crowdfunding model, rather than investing $25,000 – $1 million in a company, investors are putting in smaller amounts (think $1 – 5k).

So basically, you're getting the attention of A LOT of investors, who end up turning into your brand ambassadors. As I and other experts have said, is very ***powerful***.

How well has it worked for crowdfunding platforms?

As a platform, you can either raise funds for startups under Regulation CF or Regulation A+ of the Jobs Act. Regulation CF of the Jobs Act was put into effect in May of 2016. One year later, over $36 million has been funded through these new rules, as reported by Crowdfundinsider. The major Regulation CF platforms include:

- Wefunder – $20.4 million

- StartEngine – $7.9 million

- Indiegogo (Microventures) – $3.2 million

- NextSeed – $2.8 million

According to the WeFunder statistics, as of 2017, there have been over 50,000 successful investments in the marketplace and 164 successful offerings over $50k.

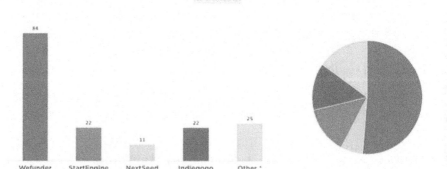

There have been **164** successful offerings over $50k

Companies that have reached a minimum funding target above $50,000

See all companies

In total, this is about $34 million in total funding in the first year. If we were to compare this to a rewards-based crowdfunding website like Kickstarter, the team raised ~$27 million in their first full year of launching their platform and $99 million in 2011.

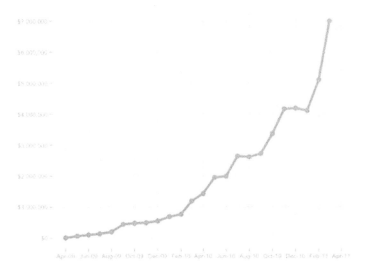

While $34 million in total funding under Regulation CF might appear dismal in comparison to VC or Angel funding, it's important to remember that massive new trends start small. We'll be able to tell just how much Regulation CF catches on in the next couple of years.

Startups have also used Regulation A+ to raise money from non-accredited retail investors. These have been referred to as mini-IPOs. This has been available since June of 2015.

According to an sec white-paper, *"Between June 19, 2015, and October 31, 2016, issuers in 147 offerings sought up to $2.6 billion in financing, including up to $1.5 billion across 81 qualified offerings. Approximately $190 million has been raised during that period, and the average issuer was seeking approximately $18 million."*

As you can see, Regulation A+ has raised more money than Regulation CF and the average raise has been larger. I'll go more into **why** when I talk about how these two raises differ. It's important to note that Regulation A+ has also been used to raise money for real estate offerings, not just startup ventures.

While Regulation CF and Regulation A+ have gotten the most attention in the startup world as of late, you can also raise money for a startup under Regulation D (506b or 506c). This is similar to a traditional offering to angel investors.

How does equity crowdfunding work for investors?

As an investor, there are limitations regarding which types of offerings you can invest in.

I know, it sucks, but that's the rules!

The major limitation is on the status of YOU as an investor. Mainly, are you an accredited or un-accredited investor?

An "accredited investor" is simply a fancy way to say that you're a high net worth individual and can afford a financial loss. While there is more to the definition, in general, accredited investors must have an annual income of $200,000 for the last two years with expectation that this will continue into the future. They could also have more than a $1 million net worth (excluding their house).

This is roughly 8.25% of American households or 10,108,811 people who qualify according to the Federal Reserve (2013).

I find it *hilarious* that the term has nothing to do with your savvy as an investor and rather with your ability to absorb a loss.

Now... non-accredited investors (most of you reading this) can invest in Regulation CF offerings AND Regulation A+ offerings. However, you cannot invest in Reg D offerings.

The reason that equity crowdfunding is getting a ton of press is because previously, most startups raised money under Regulation D. These investments were reserved for the ultra-wealthy.

Now, ANYONE can invest in a startup company before it goes onto the public stock market.

Cool, eh?

The only other thing I'd point out before we get into how this works for startups is that there are some rules guiding when you can SELL the shares that you purchase. These vary depending on the type of offering.

The rules are more comprehensive, but in general, Reg CF offerings require you to hold them for a year. You can sell them instantly under Regulation A+.

How does equity crowdfunding work for startups?

This is really where many of the differences come into play, particularly when it comes to:

- The financial costs of doing the offering
- How you can broadcast the offering
- The amount of money you can raise
- Ongoing reporting requirements

Let's start with the legal fees. According to Amy Wan on CrowdfundInsider, the legal fees for doing a Regulation A+ offering are hovering at about $100,000 per filing, exclusive of blue sky and auditing fees.

"At least two issuers spent approximately $500,000 on legal fees—one with a large law firm and another with a smaller law firm. For the most part, the legal fees are about what one would expect, with national and big law firms charging in the $150,000 – $300,000 range for representation, and smaller law firms generally charging less (although there are some notable exceptions)."

With Regulation A+, you can raise upwards of $50 million in a 12-month period under Tier II and $20 million under Tier I. Tier II requires more federal requirements but exempts you from a state-level review of your offering docs.

The great thing about Regulation A+ is that for the most part, you can freely promote the offering. You can also do a test-the-waters period to collect non-binding indications of interest and see who'd be interested in investing in the startup.

A Regulation CF offer differs a little bit, because you can only raise $1 million within a 12-month period. In addition, you are confined to basic tombstone style advertisements which direct viewers to the funding portal for more info.

Unfortunately, a Reg CF offering comes with reporting and compliance costs, which I'll go into in the next chapter. You can expect a Title III raise to cost you between $50,000 - $150,00 in legal fees.

For a short description of the various types of equity crowdfunding, see the explanation below.

Types of Equity

Equity I: A type I raise uses Rule 506 of Regulation D. It allows a company to raise unlimited capital but prohibits advertising or general solicitation. These are private platforms that only allow self-identified accredited investors, who must go through a waiting period before investing. 35 other investors are allowed, but they must at least be considered 'sophisticated investors' who understand the risks involved.

Equity II: A type II raise uses Rule 506(c). This rule allows companies to raise unlimited capital with the use of advertising and general solicitation. In turn, the platform must take responsibility for verifying that their investors are accredited, "which could include reviewing documentation, such as W-2s, tax returns, bank and brokerage statements, credit reports and the like," according to the SEC.

Equity III: A type III raise or Title III equity crowdfunding allows companies to raise a maximum of $1 million in a 12-month period. It is the only option that allows more unaccredited investors.

Regulation A+: Regulation A+ allows companies to raise up to $20 million for Tier 1 or $50 million compared to only $5 million under Regulation A. Regulation A+ offering have to submit their statements to the SEC electronically on EDGAR. All companies must complete required disclosures (using a combination of forms 1-A, S-1 and S-11) and provide independently audited financial statements. Offering statements need to be approved by the SEC before companies can make any sales under Regulation A+.

Overall, Tier II of a Regulation A+ offer has the most reporting requirements, but it allows you to raise more money. At the same time, CF and Tier I are less hassle. This might make a Reg A+ offer a better fit for an established company and a Reg CF offering a better fit for a young startup.

Pros and Cons of Equity Crowdfunding

As you now know, equity crowdfunding lets early stage companies raise investments from a 'crowd' of investors. In turn, investors get shares in startups that are not yet listed on the stock market. If the company does well, investors earn profits.

This is great because it gives small innovative companies easier access to capital. They get the funds they need and have more freedom to pursue their vision.

Even though they lose out on some of the expertise that traditional investors can offer, platforms provide tons of resources and have partnerships that benefit the startups that they work with.

Keep in mind that early stage businesses make for high risk and high reward investments. They should form part of a diversified investor portfolio to protect against illiquidity, loss of investment, and dilution.

When it comes to investing in businesses, there is never a guarantee. The truth is that most startups fail. To protect themselves, investors considering early stage businesses should focus on industries where they have experience and diversify with other investment types.

Most early-stage equity investments have historically been made by VCs and angel investors, who have experience with investing and business. Now, that privilege has been expanded to include both accredited and unaccredited investors on some platforms.

Equity Crowdfunding for Startups

For high-potential startups that need investors to get to the next level, equity crowdfunding is available in most places in the US and Europe. Even though it can be an expensive process, equity crowdfunding lets you raise investments in a whole new way and puts the power of the crowd behind you.

You will need a plan or business model with information on your company, current traction, market validation, and how you intend to maximize your investment.

To put together a Private Placement Memorandum (also referred to as an offering document), a legal document provided to investors when a company sells stocks or securities.

Pros

- Access to capital and platform resources
- Faster growth

- More freedom than when only a few investors own more equity

- Popularity, attention from investors who will want to promote your company online and help you succeed

- Requires fewer regulations and disclosures than an IPO

Cons

- These investors have less experience than Angels of VCs, who often offer mentorship and advice to companies that they invest in

- Can be a lengthy and expensive process. Companies must still make a lot of disclosures

- It can be hard managing the expectations of investors you won't meet in person, because generally equity crowdfunding keeps the platform as an intermediary

- If something goes wrong, you have more investors and more questions to answer

- Preparations for this type of crowdfunding can cost anywhere from $6K to $20K, with additional costs including audited financials (if you're raising over $500K)

Equity Crowdfunding for Investors

As you know, with equity crowdfunding, investors get access to high-risk high-reward investments and can support startups with low minimum investments, from the comfort of their homes! Since the passing of Title III crowdfunding, now even unaccredited investors can take part in equity investments online (with some restrictions, of course). These restrictions will be outlined in greater detail in chapter 2.

Accredited investors: A net worth of $1 million USD excluding the value of your primary residence or an income over $200K for 2+ years. A combined income of $300K is required for married couples.

Unaccredited investors: If an unaccredited investor's income is less than $200K, they can invest $2K or no more than 5% of their net income per year.

When investing in a company online, investors can earn returns in a few different ways.

Dividends: Money that is received based on the amount of equity an investor owns. Dividends rarely diminish the value of stock, they are simply payouts as a reward for financial support. Compared to traditional investing, communication and payouts are completed through the platform and not the startup itself.

Trade sale: If a startup you have invested in is bought by another company, you will receive a payout based on the amount of equity you own.

Public offering: If a company invested in becomes highly successful and is listed on a public stock exchange, shares can be sold at a predetermined price.

Pros

- Open and transparent process
- Easy way to diversify investments
- Earn returns
- Invest in innovative, early stage companies

Cons

- Less control than if you were one of the only investors

- Securities generally can't be sold for at least one year
- High risk

Equity Crowdfunding Statistics in 2017

In 2017, equity crowdfunding exploded onto the scene as a new way to get funding for a startup company. There's been a lot of hype by platforms, industry experts, and entrepreneurs, claiming that this new financial industry will re-define how early-stage startups link up with investors

There's no doubt that equity crowdfunding is here to stay. Already, many companies have used the new laws outlined by the Jobs Act to raise millions of dollars from the crowd. I want to get down the get down to brass tacks and share the current statistics for equity crowdfunding. We'll discuss how much funding has been raised under the various types of crowdfunding and also the future implications.

I want to talk about the first 100 equity crowdfunding campaigns that were launched under Title III of the Jobs Act (aka Reg CF). **Millyard Tech Law** did some great work here compiling this data from the US SEC EDGAR online filing system. This data set spans May 2016 – September 2016. This information will help us set the stage going forward when it comes to the type of companies that are using Reg CF.

Summarized, here are some of the findings

- *33%* fall into mobile app/internet services
- *8%* included beer and spirit companies (oddly high)
- All industries were represented
- *60%* were in business **one year or less**
- A majority were in pre-revenue stage

- Valuation caps ranged from $1.5 – $4 million

- Platform transaction fees ranged from 3-10%

- WeFunder hosted 40% of the campaigns.

- 28% of campaigns that opened in May of 2016 hit their goal (though many exceeded their fundraising minimum)

At this point in the timeframe, it's easy to see how regulation CF is being used by early-stage companies. The first 100 campaigns give some idea of the industries these startups fall into. Reg CF was put into effect in May of 2016. Since then, more than 300 startup companies filed offerings with the SEC.

Throughout this first year:

- 43% of companies received funding

- More than $40 million in capital was invested in companies

- Average campaign raised $280k from 300+ investors.

- Top platforms include: WeFunder ($18M), Start Engine ($7.4M), MicroVentures ($3.1M), NextSeed ($2.8M), and SeedInvest ($2.7M).

While $40 million doesn't come anywhere close to angel investment or venture capital statistics, it demonstrates that *real startups* are raising money using this new law. Let's talk a bit about how 2016 compares with 2017.

2017 was an epic year for Reg CF, with lots of growth and many successful campaigns. Below, I'll summarize some of the major takeaways between these two years. This is public information.

- Offerings increased from *178 in 2016* to *481 in 2017.*

- Total investment grew from *$27 million in 2016* to *$49 million in 2017.*

- Funded offerings grew from **99 in 2016** to **200 in 2017.**

- Campaigns are being launched mainly in California, Texas, Massachusetts, and New York.

Basically, the total funding under Reg CF is growing. It grew by about 267% from 2016 to 2017. Technically, 2017 is the first calendar year that this new regulation has been in effect. If equity crowdfunding were to continue to experience this level of growth, it could grow into a billion-dollar industry in the next 5 years!

Regulation A+ was put into effect on June 2015, which is about a year earlier than Reg CF of the Jobs Act.

About 16 months in (Nov 2016), the SEC commissioned a white-paper to analyze how the law was performing.

Here are some of the summarized bullet points from this report:

- Tier 2 offerings account for 60% of total offerings

- 80% of offerings did not do test-the-waters campaigns

- ~$190 million was raised between June 2015 and Oct 2016.

- Reg A+ offerings surpassed Reg A, but not Reg D offerings.

- Legal costs were ~$50,000 per offering

- Auditing costs were ~$15,000 per offering

- 121 days from filing to tier 2 qualification

- 13% of the offerings were from real estate companies

- Average issuer was seeking $18 million

- Underwriters were involved in approximately 18% of all offerings.

At the time of writing, more than $300 million has been transacted under Reg A+. Now that we've covered Reg A+ and Reg CF, let's talk about Reg D.

There is a great report that the SEC put together regarding Regulation D activity from 2010 to 2015. In 2015, more than $1.25 trillion was listed in Reg D offerings. In 2016, as compiled by CrowdfundInsider, this number hit $2 trillion.

(https://www.sec.gov/info/smallbus/acsec/private-securities-offerings-post-jobs-act-bauguess-022516.pdf)

Keep in mind that "funds offered" are different than "funds raised." Just because there was an offering does not mean that capital was secured.

In total, there were 23,292 offerings in 2016. Wow!

Based on historical information for Reg D 506(b) and 506(c) campaigns, Reg D is still the primary method of funding for startup companies when it comes to the Jobs Act. I think that in the next several years, we're going to continue to see growth in terms of the number of companies that perform Reg CF offerings. This would be accelerated if the cap on Reg CF offerings was raised (it's currently at $1,070,000).

I also believe that we're going to continue to see growth when it comes to companies using the new Reg A+ laws, particularly among real estate crowdfunding websites like Fundrise. Hopefully, more broker-dealers will also get in on this. In addition to vetting high quality companies, the success of this industry rests on the quality of education that is available to entrepreneurs, investors, and platforms.

I believe this is MY role in the process. That's one of the reasons that I am committed to putting out more quality information on equity crowdfunding!

Overall, this section gives you an idea of the pros and cons of equity crowdfunding for startups and investors. Without a doubt, there is a tremendous potential for equity crowdfunding to revolutionize the way that companies are funded. This new financial tool gives investors unprecedented access to startup companies, and the ability to invest in the next Amazon, Google, or Uber before it reaches the public stock market.

Already, millions of dollars have been transacted through equity crowdfunding platforms, leading to an explosion in the number of service providers catering to this new niche. In the next few years, we're going to see more and more companies entering this industry to help with compliance, reporting, marketing, funding, and more.

In the next few chapters, I'll be going into detail regarding how to actually get started with equity crowdfunding and the legal ramifications that you should be aware of. We'll discuss how to market an offering, attract investors, present a killer pitch, and more. As you go through this book, I would appreciate it if you took a second to leave a positive review on Amazon so that others know that this guide is worth a read. Thank you!

Chapter 2: Laws, Legal Issues, and Regulations

There are many legal implications attached to an equity crowdfunding raise. From Regulation A+ to Regulation CF, it can quickly become extremely confusing and difficult to sort out the legal mumbo jumbo.

If you're looking for a summary of how all of these laws, rules, and regulations apply to YOU, then you're in the right place.

I got you! It's an exciting time to be alive. There are so many excellent equity crowdfunding websites that it's difficult to choose from!

By the end of this chapter, I want you to have a better idea of where to get started with equity crowdfunding and what you'll need to do to comply with the various regulations. I am not a lawyer or an accountant. This chapter is not meant to construe legal or tax advice, but rather summarize my knowledge of the subject.

3 Types of Equity Crowdfunding Raises

First of all, there are three types of equity crowdfunding raises. Depending on which type that you use, the compliance requirements, costs, and benefits will be different.

#1. Regulation A+ Offering

The Jobs Act revised how Reg A offerings work. They are now referred to as "Reg A+" to reflect the new features. If someone is saying Reg A or Reg A+, they are probably referring to the same type of raise.

A Reg A+ offering falls under Title IV of the Jobs Act. Under Title IV, there are two types of financial raises, including Tier 1 and Tier 2.

Tier 1 Raise

You can raise upwards of $20 million in a 12-month period, including no more than $6 million on behalf of selling security holders that are affiliates of the issuer. These funds can be raised from both ordinary and accredited investors.

Tier 1 offerings must meet the Blue Sky investing regulations of each state that an investor resides in. You can find state-by-state filing requirements here:

(http://www.nasaa.org/industry-resources/corporation-finance/coordinated-review/regulation-a-offerings/state-filing-requirements/)

Basically, this means:

- Raise $20 million in 12 months
- Open to ordinary and accredited investors
- Must meet Blue Sky investing regulations in each investor's state

Tier 2 Raise

You can raise upwards of $50 million in a 12-month period, including no more than $15 million on behalf of selling security holders that are affiliates of the issuer. These funds can come from ordinary or accredited investors.

Tier 2 offerings preempt the Blue Sky Laws, meaning that you don't have to worry about state-by-state regulations. On the downside, there are costly reporting requirements, including audited financials and post-offering reporting.

Under both the Tier 1 and Tier 2 raise, companies can undergo a "test the waters" period to gauge the demand of investors. Investors can submit non-binding indications of interest in the offering.

This test the water period is part of Rule 225. You can publicize the test the waters offering via your social media channels and other methods.

Basically, this means:

- Raise $50 million in 12 months
- Open to ordinary and accredited investors
- Preempt the Blue Sky Laws (woo hoo!)
- Audited financials and post-offering reporting
- Can do a test the waters period to gauge demand

On the SEC website, you can find a full guide of the SEC's Amendments to Regulation A.

#2. Regulation D Offering

Regulation D offerings are the standard form of crowdfunding that existed before the Jobs Act rules were put into effect. They are also how you traditionally raise money for a startup.

When people in the industry cite Regulation D, they are referring to rule 506(b) and 506(c). They are also more likely to refer to these offerings as "private placements."

Reg D Rule 506(b)

Rule 506(b) under Regulation D is how offerings were traditionally conducted before the Jobs Act came along. They allow you to raise as much money as you'd like from Accredited Investors and up to 35 other purchasers.

While investors don't have to verify their accredited status, companies must only offer securities to buyers that are accredited. Companies cannot also advertise the offering publicly.

Reg D Rule 506(c)

Rule 506(c) was created as a result of the Jobs Act. It's a new rule that you can use to also raise money from Accredited investors. It has many of the same stipulations as 506(b), with one major difference.

You are allowed to advertise that you're raising capital under Rule 506(c). You don't need to have a prior relationship with the investors that you're getting funding from. This is referred to as "general solicitation."

Unlike Rule 506(b), you must verify that each investor is accredited before allowing them to participate in the offering.

Summarized, Reg D means that you:

- Can raise as much capital as you'd like from Accredited investors and up to 35 non-accredited investors.
- Under 506(c) you'll be able to advertise the offering
- Under 506(c) you must verify accredited investor status

On the SEC website, you can find a nitty gritty explanation of Regulation D.

#3. Title III or Regulation CF Offering

A Title III offering, also referred to as Regulation Crowdfunding or Reg CF is the long-awaited portion of the Jobs Act that enables non-accredited investors to purchase shares in startups.

Under a Title III offering, you can *raise upwards of $1,070,000* in 12-month period from ordinary investors. There are also limits in terms of how much an individual can invest, which I discuss more later in this section.

As with a traditional crowdfunding campaign, each startup must disclose information about the company like officers and directors, how the funding will be used, the fundraising period, and more.

The reporting requirements will vary depending on the amount of funding that you are seeking. Below, I'll provide a short summary of how these tiers differ.

- **$107,000 or less:** financial statements and tax returns (unless audited/reviewed financials are given)

- **$535,000 or less:** financial statements reviewed by an accountant (unless audited/reviewed financials are given).

- **$535,000 or more:** for first time offerors, financial statements reviewed by an accountant (unless audited/reviewed financials are given). For non-first time offerors, financial statements audited by a public accountant that is independent of the issuer.

Along with these stipulations, companies also have ongoing reporting requirements in the form of annual reports. Not every company is allowed to participate in a Reg CF offering. These are some of the things that could disqualify you:

- non-U.S. companies

- companies that have failed to comply with the annual reporting requirements

- companies that have no specific business plan or plan to engage in a merger or acquisition with an unidentified company or companies.

After you file your Form C with the SEC, then you can broadcast the offer. But, there are a lot of requirements regarding what you can and can't say. Some of these include:

- You can't say the terms of the offering
- Can post communications with the tombstone information
- Can say you are doing an offering under Section 4(a)(6), as long as it doesn't mention the terms.
- Drive investors to the intermediary's website to find out more.
- Think tombstone advertisements (only factual info)

For more information about Title III, you can view the SEC's website.

These are the three main types of equity crowdfunding. In an article, I've covered the topic of Instrastate Crowdfunding, which is a whole other discussion:

See: crowdcrux.com/intrastate-crowdfunding-now/

Filing and Disclosure Requirements

In order to do an equity crowdfunding offering, you're going to face a bunch of filing and disclosure requirements. These rules are primarily there to protect investors.

These requirements are going to vary based on the type of crowdfunding that you choose to use. Regulation CF requirements will be different from Regulation A+.

To help clarify this confusing part of the fundraising process, I'm going to break down the various forms and filing procedures by funding type. Of course, you should do your own research, but I hope this helps you with the process.

Regulation A+ Form

It takes time to be approved by the SEC for a Reg A+ raise. You can expect that it will take about 60 days to compile, answer, and submit the necessary forms and information to the SEC. Then, it can take anywhere from 30-60 days to get approval for the offering.

- You must complete Form 1-A, which is the offering form for Reg A+ of the Jobs Act.

- You can submit Form 1-A online through EDGAR. You can print a physical copy here:

  https://www.sec.gov/files/form1-a.pdf

- You must complete all questions/fields and provide audited financial statements.

Regulation D 506(c) Form

The good news is that there are no Regulation D 506(c) forms that you need to fill out before raising money. You do not have to register your offering of securities with the SEC.

Once you do successfully sell your securities to Accredited Investors, you must file a Form D on EDGAR (or a print version here: https://www.sec.gov/files/formd.pdf) within 15 calendar days after you finish your securities sale.

Regulation Crowdfunding Form

As with the other types of crowdfunding, it does take time to prepare for a Reg CF raise. You must fill out paperwork in order to educate investors and the public about the offering.

When doing a regulation crowdfunding offering, you must:

- File Form C on EDGAR and make it public (prior to start of offering). Here's a print version:

  https://www.sec.gov/files/formc.pdf

- Financial statements, as detailed earlier

- Ongoing disclosure in the form of annual reporting (but need not be audited or reviewed by an accountant). The entity must continue to file annual reports unless they fall into a few different categories, as outlined on the SEC website.

Investor Limitations and Rules

There are limitations on the amount that investors can invest when it comes to an equity crowdfunding campaign. As with the other sections, these limitations and rules vary depending on the type of crowdfunding that you choose.

These rules are there to help protect investors against massive financial losses. They are important to know if you're a platform, company, or service provider in the crowdfunding industry.

Regulation A+ Investors

For Reg A+, both accredited and non-accredited investors can buy shares during your offering. There is one important difference when it comes to Reg A+!

Under Tier 1 offerings, investors have no limitations regarding the amount of money that they can invest.

However, under Tier 2 offerings, non-accredited investors can only invest 10% of their annual income or net worth per year (whichever is greater).

Regulation D 506(c) Investors

When doing a Reg D 506(b) or 506(c) offering, there aren't any investors limitations regarding the amount that they can invest.

The only limitation is that this type of offering is only available to Accredited Investors (and a small handful of non-accredited investors).

Regulation Crowdfunding Investors

Regulation CF probably has the most limitations on investors of all of the types of equity crowdfunding that we've mentioned thus far.

These limitations come in the form of the amount that you can invest in a 12-month period and they are determined by your annual income or net worth (the greater of the two). Your house is not included in your net worth.

According to the SEC website, "If *either* your annual income *or* your net worth is less than $107,000, then during any 12-month period, you can invest up to the greater of either $2,200 or 5% of the lesser of your annual income or net worth.

If *both* your annual income *and* your net worth are equal to or more than $107,000, then during any 12-month period, you can invest up to 10% of annual income or net worth, whichever is lesser, but not to exceed $107,000."

I will cut and paste an example chart from the SEC website below.

Annual Income	Net Worth	Calculation	12-month Limit
$30,000	$105,000	greater of $2,200 or 5% of $30,000 ($1,500)	$2,200
$150,000	$80,000	greater of $2,200 or 5% of $80,000 ($4,000)	$4,000
$150,000	$107,000	10% of $107,000 ($10,000)	$10,700
$200,000	$900,000	10% of $200,000 ($20,000)	$20,000
$1.2 million	$2 million	10% of $1.2 million ($120,000), subject to cap	$107,000

As I mentioned previously, a Reg CF offering is available for both accredited and non-accredited investors.

Platform Regulations

Lastly, when it comes to the equity crowdfunding laws, there are the regulations that the US government places on the actual websites, platforms, or portals that you can use to launch a crowdfunding campaign.

Regulation A+ Platform Requirements

Under Reg A+, a company does not need to go through a broker dealer or an intermediary to sell securities. This means that technically, a company could house a Reg A+ offering on their own website!

As a platform, you will mainly be providing a marketplace of investors that new companies can tap into, along with helping them with the process of doing a Reg A+ offering or test the waters campaign.

Regulation D Platform Requirements

Similar to Reg A+, a startup doesn't have to go through a broker dealer to do a Reg D offering. Depending on the type of offering (whether it's 506(b) or 506(c)), the company might already be in touch with the investors or they plan to broadcast the campaign online.

As a platform, you can offer a website where startups can connect with investors under a 506(c) offering. This is the type of offering that many crowdfunding platforms started to feature in the early stages of the Jobs Act.

Regulation CF Platform Requirements

Finally, there are Reg CF offerings, which have a few more requirements than the prior two. In order to function as a platform, you must become a registered funding portal and member of FINRA. You can follow the step-by-step process here:

(http://www.finra.org/industry/register-new-funding-portal)

Broker dealers can also do Reg CF offerings.

According to the SEC website, "A registered funding portal is prohibited from:

- Offering investment advice or recommendations;

- Soliciting purchases, sales or offers to buy the securities displayed on its platform;

- Compensating employees, agents, or other persons for such solicitation or based on the sale of securities displayed or referenced on its platform; or

- Holding, managing, possessing, or handling investor funds or securities."

If you plan to do any of the above, then you'll need to register as a broker dealer, not a crowdfunding portal.

The process for applying to become a registered crowdfunding portal is as follows:

1. Reserve your firm's name with FINRA

2. File with the SEC

3. Complete FINRA entitlement form

4. Submit finger prints

5. Pay application fees

6. FINA will assess application (within 14 days)

7. Examination of application/requests for changes

8. Interview of applicant

9. FINRA decision.

Other Risks Involved...

Now that you have a clearer idea of how equity crowdfunding works from a rules and regulation standpoint, I want to introduce you to some of the risks for investors, startups, and platforms. I'm not trying to scare you, but rather make you aware of potential downsides before you make the leap!

The next chapter will be an honest overview of the top equity crowdfunding websites out there. I'll share with you what you need to be aware of when it comes to this alternative financial tool and the differences between these sites.

Chapter 3: Best Equity Crowdfunding Websites

In the previous chapters, we've discussed what equity crowdfunding is, how you can use it, and some of the legal requirements for an online funding round. Now, let's get into the good stuff! The platforms that you can actually use to raise money from the crowd. These are the websites or portals that you will use to host your equity crowdfunding campaign.

As you've seen, there are different types of equity crowdfunding, including Reg CF, Reg A+, and Reg D. Depending on your resources, preferences, and the stage of your startup, you might gravitate to one over the other. In the same way that there are different forms of crowdfunding, there are also platforms that are leaders in *one area,* but *not leaders* in another.

For example, an equity crowdfunding website could be really good at Reg CF campaigns, but they might struggle when it comes to handling a Reg A+ financial raise. This could quite simply be due to their deal flow, but it could also get into their investor marketplace, their marketing strategy, and their own skills or abilities. While I'll be recommending that you check out a few of the top equity crowdfunding platforms out there, it's important to keep in mind that there is no one leader in the industry (as of yet).

1. WeFunder

WeFunder is one of the top equity crowdfunding websites out there! In the section covering crowdfunding statistics, I outlined how they comprised 40% of the initial 100 Reg CF campaigns.

It's crystal clear that this equity crowdfunding platform is leading the pack when it comes to Regulation Crowdfunding campaigns. I want to discuss some of the pros and cons of using their website, along with some of the statistics and information that you might not be familiar with.

If you're entrepreneur or startup founder, then I'm sure you've seen some of the different funding portals that are out there and might be wondering... is WeFunder a good fit for you?

One year into the enactment of Reg CF, WeFunder was responsible for $18 million in terms of their funding volume. This makes them the leader of the pack for Reg CF. The company has also put together their own statistics when it comes to the companies that have raised money on their platform. According to the website, more than $50 million has been transacted at the time of writing.

More than 182 companies have raised money under Reg CF on the platform and there have been more than 60,000 investments that have been made. It's evident that WeFunder has done very well with Reg CF, though they haven't seen the same level of success with other funding structures like Reg A+ and Reg D. According to the company website, 73% of the startups that launched campaigns were successfully funded.

The fees that come with using WeFunder are going to vary depending on the type of funding you're doing. Basically, this refers to the regulation of the Jobs Act that you're using.

- **Regulation Crowdfunding (Title III):** Investors will be charged up to 2% of their investment minimum and companies will be charged up to 7% of their total funding amount.

- **Regulation A+:** There are no fees to do a Regulation A+ campaign on WeFunder.

- **Regulation D:** The website will charge up to 20% of carried interest, which is basically a share of the future profits from the financial raise. When the startup experiences a liquidation event, like an acquisition or an IPO, WeFunder will get a portion of those funds.

As you can see, the costs that you experience as a startup company are going to vary. This is true across other crowdfunding platforms as well. WeFunder also charges a $195 fee before your campaign goes live.

If you're interested in using WeFunder to conduct your equity crowdfunding campaign, then I'm going to hook you up with a massive $1,000 discount!

When your fundraising campaign closes, you'll get $1,000 off WeFunder's fundraising fees. You just gotta use this special link to set up your campaign:

http://www.crowdcrux.com/wefunder

After you click through, you just gotta fill out your company information, get everything sorted out, file your Form C, and then you're ready to go! (This is an affiliate link.)

The great thing about WeFunder is that it's open to both accredited and non-accredited investors! Unless the startup is doing a Reg D raise, you'll be able to invest in the companies on this platform.

The amount of money that you'll be able to invest will vary depending on the regulations that the startup is using to raise money. For example, under regulation crowdfunding, everyone can invest at least $2,200. If your net worth or income are above $107k, you can invest a maximum of 10% of the lesser number.

Finally, both US and International investors are allowed to participate on this platform.

While there are many benefits, I also think there are tons of downsides to using WeFunder. For one thing, if you're doing a Reg

D offering, you're giving away a ton of equity to the platform when you sell your company or go public.

Second of all, you're giving away a good chunk of your financial raise when using their platform under Regulation CF. You also gotta pay a fee before it goes live. It's pretty common knowledge that you can't only rely on the investors in their marketplace. You also gotta promote your own project. You gotta invest in a marketing and PR campaign for our offering.

I think WeFunder is offering a lot when it comes to the functionality, ease-of-use, and how they help you with the contracts related to an equity crowdfunding raise.

2. Start Engine.

Start Engine is one of the top equity crowdfunding platforms out there that you can use to either raise money from the crowd or invest in cool new startups.

The website was started in 2011 and has gone on to amass more than 80,000 users, of which more than 15,000 have made investments on their platform. In total, the company has helped startups raise more than $35 million from the public.

I've had the team behind this platform on my podcast several times to discuss crowdfunding. They've been very helpful when it comes to educating investors, entrepreneurs, and the media. This is sorely needed in the crowdfunding space.

I want to go into the pros and cons of raising money on StartEngine, along with some of the details that you'll need to know and costs that you'll incur. No matter what stage your startup is in, I hope that you find this section to be helpful!

StartEngine allows both accredited and non-accredited investors to discover startups on their platform. If you're an entrepreneur, you can do a Reg CF (small public offering), Reg A+

(large public offering) campaign, or an ICO using their software and marketplace.

Under a Reg CF campaign, you can raise upwards of $1.07 million in a 12 month period and under Reg A+, you can raise upwards of $50 million in a 12 month period.

You must be a US-based company to be able to raise funds on the site. You must also fit the platform requirements. For the most part, the companies that have raised money fall into tech, food & beverage, medical, hospitality, communications, and other industries.

Depending on which funding type you choose, the process will be different. In general, you must create a campaign page, meet the compliance requirements (which may or may not require a lawyer/accountant), and then set up a marketing strategy to get the word out.

What are the fees and costs related to doing a campaign with this platform? StartEngine charges a variety of fees for equity crowdfunding campaigns, which depends on the type of crowdfunding that you go with. These fees help to finance the cost of running the platform and marketing it to more investors.

Small online offerings: 6% fee of the capital raised for a Small OPO (also known as Reg CF campaign). The entrepreneur will pay this fee.

Large online offering: $50/unique investor + warrants OR a $20,000/month + warrants hosting fee. A large OPO is the same as a Reg A+ offering.

Full Service Support (consulting, creative services, on-boarding): $5,000/campaign. This includes access to more support infrastructure that will help your company be more successful.

Investor Management: $3,000/year to enroll in the investor management system, StartEngine Secure.

As you can see, there are platform-related costs associated with doing an equity crowdfunding campaign, which vary based on the level of support and assistance that you're seeking.

If you're raising under $100,000, you can get away with minimal costs for the campaign, because you only need to provide the financial information from your tax returns, which is certified by the principal executive officer.

Who can invest on StartEngine? Both accredited and non-accredited investors can invest in the offerings on the StartEngine marketplace. This is because the startups are doing Reg CF or Reg A+ financial raises.

You can look around at the various companies that are raising money, watch their videos, get access to their pitch deck, learn about their background, and get into the details of the actual offering.

You can see one example campaign below, which has raised over $900,000 under Title III of the Jobs Act (Reg CF) and has 32 days left in the fundraising period. The minimum investment is $400.

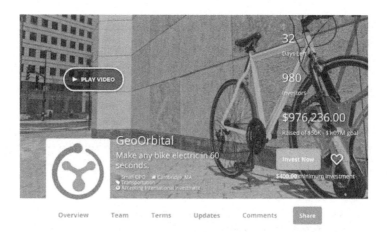

When you put this project up there, you are inviting people from around the world to discover what your product is, who your management team is, and learn about your overarching mission. You should expect **public comments** from the investment community.

Some of these comments will be related to your product or people looking to help your startup, like the examples below. Some will be from investors or potential investors.

Samuel Jackson GeoOrbital · Potential Investor a month ago
Hi i invest about three month ago i wanted to know how can i become a saleman for your company to make sales to police department

> GeoOrbital StartEngine GeoOrbital · Issuer 22 days ago
> @ Samuel Jackson thank you for being an investor! Please reach out to us directly on our website.

Tricia Richards-Smith GeoOrbital · Potential Investor 2 months ago
Are you going to make it for 20 inch wheels at some point in product lifecycle?

> GeoOrbital StartEngine GeoOrbital · Issuer a month ago
> @Tricia Richards-Smith we will be making smaller sized wheels later on, but unfortunately the market for wheel sized under 26 inches is more limited a the moment.

Naturally, as a byproduct of being public with your company, you might also get criticism. People might question your decisions. You're going to have to communicate the steps related to your business and business-related customer service.

Going into your project, you should have a plan for investor management and how you're going to approach questions, concerns, and inquiries.

So, who can raise money on StartEngine?

In order to raise funds on StartEngine, your company must be based in the United States and be a legal entity (LLC, C Corp). You must also meet the standard requirements for doing a Reg CF or Reg A+ raise.

The website has a variety of forbidden company categories, some of which include weaponry, marijuana, and tobacco.

Lastly, to be listed on the website, you gotta pass a Bad Actor background check and the standard review process for the crowdfunding platform.

Some of the industries that have raised money on the website include:

- Food and beverage
- Technology
- Health and beauty
- Sports and fitness

- Education

- Mobile app

- Automotive

- Medical, and more.

Now that we've gone into some of the details of this particular platform, let's talk about its reach and size. In 2017, StartEngine did $2.1 million in annual revenue, which was generated from success fees, events, sponsorships, StartEngine Secure/Premium, and more. The company also hosted 61 successful campaigns (as opposed to 6 in 2016).

2015 Revenue: $222k

2016 Revenue: $308k

2017 Revenue: $2.1 M

A lot of their revenue in 2017 came from their ancillary services that are there to help entrepreneurs with the fundraising process. About $701k came from StartEngine Secure, StartEngine Premium, events and sponsorships, licensing services, and transactional services. The reason why StartEngine is sharing all of this information is because they are actually in the middle of a live offering under Title IV of the Jobs Act. Basically, you can own equity in the platform if you'd like.

In 2017, WeFunder was the clear leader when it came to the volume of equity crowdfunding campaigns launched under Regulation CF. Now, StartEngine has hosted more than 160 offerings, putting it on part with WeFunder when it comes to the volume of offerings (this is different from total funds raised).

3. Angel List

Angel List was founded in 2010 and aims to connect angel investors with tech startups. At the time of writing, the company has raised about $600 million in funds to continue its operation. As of 2015, over $160 million was raised through the website from 3k+ investors for 441 startups. Private deals were about 40% of the overall funding rounds and there were institutional funds in 40% of the rounds.

In addition to providing a marketplace where startups can connect with investors, Angel List also has a job marketplace that links up job seekers with startups hungry for new talent. There were 548K "job matches" in 2015.

Aside from the job marketplace and having a large amount of clout among investors, I think that there is one major difference that sets Angel List apart from equity crowdfunding platforms like SeedInvest. One word: syndicates.

"A syndicate allows investors to participate in a lead investor's deals. In exchange, investors pay the lead carry."

Basically, there are professional angel investors out there who have access to deal flow and a tremendous amount of experience. Those investors can choose to lead a syndicate. In exchange, they get access to more investors for the deal and get carry. Carry is a form of compensation to the head of the investment syndicate. Simply put, it's a percentage of the fund's net profits. The lead investor usually provides about 16% of the overall capital.

"On average, syndicates charge 19.5% deal carry, which is equivalent to a 25% fund carry." – Source

On the plus side, a startup will get more capital with fewer investor interactions and back and forth communication with the lead investor.

Cost: Investors pay 0- 25% deal carry to the lead of their syndicate and 5% deal carry to AngelList Advisors, along with out-of-pocket costs. There are no management fees.

4. SeedInvest

Having launched in 2013, SeedInvest has seen a number of successful crowdfunding raises on its platform, including **KnightScope**, which topped off its Series A round and raised $1.5 million in funds in 2014, Virtuix, which raised $7.9 million from 1832 investors, and Vengo, which r**aised $720,000 of its $2 million** in funding.

At the time of writing the platform says that it has helped 70+ get funding to the tune of $50 million via 136,989 investors. The platform itself has raised its own Series A round for $4.15 million on their website.

The platform lets you invest in both Regulation A+ offerings and Crowdfunding offerings. Entrepreneurs can also do a test the waters period to gauge the public's interest in their offering. For those entrepreneurs raising under Regulation D, the *"SeedInvest Selections Fund is currently investing $200,000 alongside each company that successfully raises capital on SeedInvest[1] under Regulation D."* They are aiming to invest in 50 companies in the next 2 years.

The website actually self-funded its own Series A round for $4.15 million. According to the press release, "SeedInvest met its initial $3 million goal in only one week and accepted $1.15 million of additional commitments before ending its campaign just a week later."

The company "raised the first $2 million from prominent venture capital firms...then closed $2.15 million from forty-two angel investors through the SeedInvest platform. During the two-week campaign, over 3,000 prospective investors accessed the investment opportunity and more than 400 signed-up as new investors on the platform."

Most companies on SeedInvest are looking to raise between $100,000 – $50,000,000 and are technology or consumer-centric businesses. They should have already attracted a lead investor and set their funding terms.

Fundraising duration: 60 days minimum

Costs: "5% – 7.5% placement fee; charged on the total amount raised on SeedInvest in the round, paid only upon the successful completion of your offering.

5% warrant coverage or equity; based on the total amount raised on SeedInvest in the round.

Up to $0 – $4,000 in due diligence, escrow, marketing and legal expense reimbursements."

If you'd like to raise between $100,000 and $50,000,000 on SeedInvest, you'll need a minimum viable product, traction, a US incorporated business, and at least two full-time teammates.

Lastly, SeedInvest has an **auto-invest feature**, where you can invest in 25 stage startups through their automated investing capability. You'll be notified of new startups that launch on the platform and have access to lower invest minimums.

5. Microventures

Microventures is an equity crowdfunding platform that you can use to find startups to invest in. Entrepreneurs raise money on this site using Regulation D Rule 506 and Reg CF. This means that both accredited and non-accredited investors can check out investments on Microventures. Over $85 million has been raised on the platform.

Indiegogo is partnered with MicroVentures to offer equity crowdfunding for their website users. All of the transactions related to equity crowdfunding are done through the MicroVentures website and off Indiegogo's main website.

MicroVentures is one of the top FINRA registered broker-dealers in the equity crowdfunding space. At the time of writing, they've raised over $100 million for companies on their platform from accredited investors. Also, over 95% of the campaigns on their platform have been funded.

It's free to create an account, but you'll be paid an investment processing fee if you decide to invest in a company. Investment minimums start at $100.

While MicroVentures states that they have raised money for a bunch of different types of companies, their main areas of focus include:

- Internet Technology
- Media and Entertainment
- Software
- Green Technology
- Mobile
- Social
- Gaming

Remember that unlike rewards-based crowdfunding, you're going to be giving away shares of your company in exchange for investment. You can also decide to offer swag or rewards to your investors. For example, for the people that invested $100 in the ArtCraft Entertainment equity crowdfunding campaign, they also got:

- Access to Beta 2 and all subsequent tests
- Digital copy of *Crowfall*
- Allows you to post on the *Crowfall* forums!
- Thanks in the credits as a 2017 Patron

- 2017 Early Backer Avatar Frame

- 2017 Early Backer Forum Badge

- All 2017 Badges and Frames up to Early Backer level

If you're going to be raising funds on Indiegogo/MicroVentures, it's going to take about six weeks from the application to being fully funded. It will then take about 2 weeks to receive your funds. Remember that under Title III, you can raise upwards of $1 million in a 12 month period. You can raise between $150k – $1 million through Indiegogo/MicroVentures.

After you successfully raise funds, there will be ongoing reporting requirements. You'll have to update your investors on a quarterly basis. Considering that investors are required by the SEC to hold their investment for at least one year, you should see this as a long-term relationship, until an eventual liquidation event.

One of the big differences between MicroVentures and other funding portals is that it also functions as a FINRA registered broker-dealer.

6. CircleUp

CircleUp is an equity crowdfunding platform that you can use to raise money for your startup company online. The company started in 2010 and is headquartered in San Francisco, California. Since their launch, they've helped 256 companies raise $390 million on their platform.

CircleUp is catered towards early-stage consumer brands that have physical products (think retail). The company is a FINRA registered broker/dealer. As an entrepreneur, you can list your offering on their website, which includes access to more than 850 professional accredited investors.

Once you've submitted your application and passed rounds of due diligence, you'll gain access to CircleUp Hub and be able to work on your fundraising campaign page. This will pass a final review by the company and then you'll be able to list it on their marketplace.

On average, if you've done your job right, you should be able to hit your target investment amount within about 60 to 90 days. You must hit or exceed this minimum amount to be able to keep the funds that are raised.

The big difference between CircleUp and other equity crowdfunding websites is that they specialize in Reg D raises **under 506(c) or 506(b).** They do not allow Reg A+ or Reg CF campaigns on their platform at the time of writing.

Let's talk fees! According to the company website, CircleUp will charge a commission based on the total amount raised. In their words, the commission is comparable to "what companies pay to investment bankers in the offline world for similar size fundraising rounds."

Personally, I've found a lot of different data regarding what investment banks charge for their fundraising fees. There are different formulas to come to this number. For example, when it comes to M&A transactions, Axial reports that "the Double Lehman scale is more prevalent: 10 percent of the first million dollars, 8 percent of the second, 6 of the third, 4 of fourth and 2 of everything thereafter. Variations on the structure have also become more common, tailored to each deal."

When it comes to fundraising numbers, Global Capital Funding Group reports that, "Middle market deals classically provide for minimum success fees in the range of $250,000 to $750,000, with most minimums falling on the low side of this range...

We typically see success fees in a very competitive market starting as low as .75% for deals at the highest end of the middle market and as high as 5% at the lowest end of the middle market. Prominent middle market investment bankers with "real" industry expertise target success fees of at least $1,000,000 per transaction."

Based on my research on websites like InvestmentBank, the actual fees for a deal are extremely variable and deal-dependent. It will vary based on timing, level of preparation, deal size, and more. Some report it can vary from 3 – 5%.

I would like to see more clarity on this point from CircleUp. I would recommend researching this point more before discussing numbers with a funding portal or broker-dealer.

Who can invest on CircleUp? Since CircleUp companies are only using the Regulation D 506(b) or 506(c) rules under Title II of the Jobs Act, there are limitations on who can invest in these offerings.

You can only invest in a company on CircleUp if you are an accredited investor. What does this mean? Basically, accredited investors are wealthy individuals. They are earning $200k per year or have a $1 million net worth or more (excluding their house).

Accredited investors are not only limited to individuals. You can also qualify as one if you're an institution like a bank, insurance company, broker, or trust, then you can also invest on CircleUp. In fact, over 50% of the capital comes from institutional investors.

Since CircleUp does not have plans to do Reg CF or Reg A+ offerings, non-accredited investors cannot invest on this platform. What about entrepreneurs? Who can raise money?

This company specializes in equity campaigns for high growth product-centric or retail-oriented startups. These raises are between $1 – $5 million. Some of these industries include:

- Fashion/Apparel

- Accessories

- Pet care

- Electronics

- Restaurants

- Beauty

- Food and beverage

You must apply to be able to raise money on CircleUp. They will put you through a vetting process, where which the majority of companies are weeded out. In fact, only 7% are approved to raise money on the website.

After you're approved, you can run your campaign. There is both a fundraising minimum and maximum on this platform. You cannot raise more than the maximum on the site (though technically, Reg D has no limit).

Overall, there have been 256 companies that have successfully raised money on CircleUp to the tune of $390 million in funding.

The marketplace has access to more than 800 investors, 50% of which are institutions. When it comes to Reg D offerings, quality definitely matters more than quantity.

Along with having the marketplace. CircleUp also has a $125 million Growth Partners fund which uses their AI Helio software to identify growing startups worthy of investment. They plan to invest in starts through smaller checks of ~$400k at the rate of 35-40 investments over the next 3 years.

Seeing as institutional investors make up the Growth Partners fund, it's basically a VC operation.

7. FundersClub

FundersClub is an equity crowdfunding website that has helped more than 270 startups get funded to the tune of more than $100 million dollars.

As an entrepreneur, you can use their "online VC" website to get funding for your startup company at the series A or seed stage. As an investor, you can participate in early funding rounds of fast-growing companies.

FundersClub is a San Francisco company that was founded in 2012. They began as a new way for investors to connect with startups through an online marketplace.

Primarily, the platform is interested in early-stage technology companies seeking a seed stage or Series A funding round. You gotta have a strong team, demonstrate traction, and be going after a large market.

Since starting, FundersClub has acquired more than 19,000 members, invested in portfolio companies that have received 26 exits, and raised over $100 million in capital.

Along with providing a market to reach angel investors, FundersClub also pairs founders with more than 600 other founders and entrepreneurs. The company has extensive experience launching, growing, and exiting startups, which they pass on through on-going mentorship.

One big differentiator between FundersClub and some of the other platforms out there is that this platform only accepts angel investors (accredited investors) on their platform.

There are costs associated with doing any kind of financial raise and those that are specifically paid to FundersClub in exchange for helping with the transaction.

According to the website, FundersClub charges carried interest for the majority of its funds. As the site says, "carry is a percent of any profits from a fund."

Single company funds: carry ranges from 1 – 30% based on performance (typically 20%)

Multi company funds: carry ranges from 1 – 30% based on performance. There is also a 0.25 – 3% annual management fee which goes to the fund manager. This management fee averages to be about 0.5 – 2%.

Along with these costs, there are also administrative costs related to each fund which are set aside. This comes out to be 10%. These funds are not used for compensation.

"This fee does not dilute the startup; for example, if $250K is pledged by FundersClub members, $225K is invested in the startup, and $25K is set aside for legal and accounting costs." – Source.

FundersClub is only open to accredited investors (what does this mean?). Basically, these are people with a high yearly income and large net worth. They can afford to invest in risky startups.

Less than 2% of the companies pass through the vetting and due diligence process. You're getting access to the cream of the crop.

Of course, there are no guarantees when it comes to the returns that you can expect on their website. In my research, I found that the IRR varied from 8% net IIR to 44%. You can take a look at some of the multiples below.

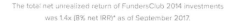

The total net unrealized return of FundersClub 2014 investments
was 1.4x (8% net IRR)* as of September 2017.

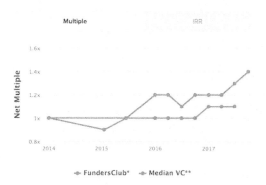

Remember that past performance is no guarantee of future results. If you wanna check out more about the returns, you can browse their site.

2012 Vintage   **2013 Vintage**   2014 Vintage   2015 Vintage

The total net unrealized return of FundersClub 2013 investments
was 4.6x (42% net IRR)* as of September 2017.

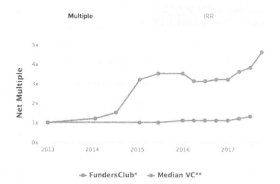

Unlike traditional investments on the public stock market, your investments on FundersClub will be illiquid. This means that your investment horizon is going to be much longer.

You'll only get a distribution when a liquidation event happens. This simply means that the startup is either acquired or goes public. This can take 4 to 7 years or longer to happen. In some cases, there might not be any kind of distribution.

The minimum to get started investing is $3,000 per fund. The average check size is going to vary depending on the type of investor. The interesting thing about this site is that the average check size is much smaller than with traditional angel investing ($25k – $250k).

So, who can raise money on FundersClub? If you want to do a funding round for your company, then listen up!

Firstly, you gotta fit into what FundersClub is looking for… they want to get a massive return for their investors, so naturally, they can't accept every company.

In general, you should expect to have:

- A world-class team that can execute on the vision, deal with the day-to-day grind, overcome obstacles, and stay ambitious.

- Product-market fit, which just a fancy way to say traction. People should be buying or using your product in a measurable way. You should be seeing growth.

- Some aspect of scale, meaning technology. Technology is there to increase automation and make it easier to scale. No scale means bad returns in a VC's eyes.

- The potential to make a lotta cash. You gotta be going after a BIG problem with a solution that addresses a BIG market.

If you got all of that, dope! You're ready to apply...

To get started, you just need to submit your application, talk with a member of the site's team, go through an investment committee review, create a profile, and then undergo a panel review.

This is the last step of the process and not many startups make it this far. According to the website, it's less than 2%!

So, how popular is FundersClub? Well, we can't really compare it to other equity crowdfunding sites doing Reg CF or Reg A+ raises. That's because this site is primarily focused on VC and angel-style investing into emerging technology startups.

You can correct me if I'm wrong, but I imagine they're probably doing 506(b) or 506(c) offerings under regulation D, which is the traditional way to raise money from angel investors for startup companies.

In this way, they'd be a bit more similar to platforms like CircleUp or AngelList. At the time of writing, FundersClub has facilitated more than $100 million in investments across more than 270 startups.

Of the companies in their portfolio, they've had 20 companies that were acquired and more than $2 billion in funds that went to companies (in later rounds) that started with FundersClub.

I find it interesting that the average check size at the five-year mark was $10,857 and the average FundersClub check size was $291,364.

The companies that have made up their portfolio come from industries like:

- IT
- Financial technology

- Health and medicine

- Retail

- Food and agriculture

- Human resources and more...

As you can see, these guys are one of the forerunners at adopting technology and bringing it to the funding game. I think we're gonna see some great progress from them in the future.

8. Crowdcube and Seedrs

Crowdcube and Seedrs are two major UK-based equity crowdfunding platforms. The reason I'm lumping them together is that I want to mention them in this list, but also, I'm not going to be covering much of equity crowdfunding outside of the United States. Seeing as the laws and regulations are so vast and vary from country to country, I'm limiting the scope of this book to companies that are raising money in the US.

At the time of writing, Crowdcube has raised more than £212m and Seeders has raised more than £190m. Crowdcube is the leader when it comes to largest campaign and number of raises and successful exits, but not by much. Overall, these two are pretty evenly matched.

I think the biggest difference comes down to the *type* of company that raises money on their platforms and the costs and fees associated with each website. For example, Seedrs historically has been a better fit for earlier stage startups. This is verified by some of the guests that I've had on my podcast. Crowdcube seems to be a better fit for startups in the mature phases. However, both sites accept startups in every form.

Second, Seeders differs from Crowdcube in its fee structure. They charge 6% on the first £150,000 raised, 4% on funds after first £150,000 and before £500,000, and finally a 2% fee for everything over £500,000. Crowdcube just charges a 7% fee on all funds raised.

While we don't have time to cover these two platforms in-depth, if you are located in the UK, I invite you to check them out on their respective websites and learn a bit about how they work. They are the leaders in their space.

9. Fundable

Fundable is an equity crowdfunding platform that you can use to raise capital or invest in startup companies online. At the time of writing, more than $411 million in funding has been committed on Fundable across a variety of different industries.

Unlike other websites, Fundable operates as both a rewards-based and equity crowdfunding website (that functions more as a database).

Rewards-based crowdfunding is similar to Kickstarter. Backers are gaining access to "perks" or "rewards" when they pledge money to your project. This could be an early version of the finished product, or an initial production run of the end product.

Equity crowdfunding is when an entrepreneur gives away shares in their company to investors who then become partial owners in the startup. It's like doing an initial public offering on the open market.

As a founder, you can offer investors equity and convertible/non-convertible debt in your startup. You'll simply create a profile, set up your terms, structure your deal, get approved, and then market your project.

Your investment will then be available for accredited investors to browse on the platform.

The important thing to note is that Fundable is not a broker dealer. As the website says, *"Legally we cannot charge fees after funding for equity. All funds transfers, final deal terms and legal documentation are worked out between the investor and company directly after the end of the fundraise off-site."*

This means that *"Any fees charged are up to the discretion of both you and the individual investor, and you can investigate methods of transferring the money between yourselves."*

Fundable operates a bit differently from some of the other equity crowdfunding websites out there. They don't take any kind of success fee or fees related to the amount that you've raised.

Instead, Fundable charge $179 per month to create and manage your fundraiser and use their platform. This is a software as a service model. You're paying to use their software and gain access to their marketplace.

Now... you might be thinking that's too good to be true, right? If you're doing a fundraising campaign for six, seven, or eight figures, traditionally, you'd expect a much more hefty fee.

In my opinion, the reason why that Fundable is able to make this model work is that they are very **hands-off** with the entire equity crowdfunding process.

They basically give you a database of people who are accredited investors and it's up to you to connect with them, market your project, and get funding.

It's up to you to figure out how to do final deal terms, legal documentation, and fund transfers. When browsing their help section, their default answer was pretty much "get legal counsel."

For rewards-based campaigns, Fundable does charge a 3.5% + $0.30 per transaction WePay fee.

So, who can invest on Fundable? Only accredited investors can invest on Fundable. You must meet the yearly income and net worth threshold. Investment minimums start at $1,000.

It's very important to note that the actual funding transaction will not happen on Fundable. It will be handled individually by the company/investors. The only thing you're doing when you "invest" on Fundable is make an investing commitment.

Basically, you're gaining access to a database of startups that are looking for funding and by expressing interest, you'll telling one of those startups that you're ready to invest in them.

When it comes to raising money, at the time of writing, only US-based companies can raise money on Fundable. You can think of the website as a skeleton of the deal that you are going to offer investors.

As it says, "Ultimately, a company's agreements with the investor and SEC fillings are what determines how much can be raised and how much can be oversubscribed."

This language leaves the deal terms pretty open, meaning that most of the work is going to happen behind the scenes with your legal counsel in drawing up documents and figuring out the details of the offering.

According to the website, more than 377,000+ entrepreneurs have joined their community and successfully raised millions in private capital from investors. The homepage states that companies have raised more than $411 million on the site.

The company that owns Fundable also owns Startups.co, Bizplan, Clarity, Launchrock, and Zirtual. It's clear that they're trying to provide an all-around solution for startups and entrepreneurs.

Personally, I would not recommend using Fundable. For all of the work that goes into an equity crowdfunding campaign, you're better off going with a platform that has its incentives more aligned with your success.

In my opinion, these guys basically give you the software to make a campaign page and a database of investors. Again, this is my opinion, but it seems to me like this platform wants to be very hands-off and that's just not practical for an equity crowdfunding campaign. You need a lot of horsepower behind the financial raise and good quality leads that aren't burnt out.

I think they're trying to get a lot of people to use their software on a monthly payment basis, as that's their business model. The things they say and do will be aligned with getting more long-term users of their software. That's not necessarily the best thing.

I also looked up some reviews of this platform and came across many that were questionable.

Which Equity Crowdfunding Site is Best?

As you can see, different platforms are catered to different types of financial raises. Some are better for one type of regulation, like Reg CF, and others are better for Reg D. The site that is best is going to vary depending on your needs as a startup company, the amount you want to raise, and your overall resources.

I would first examine how much you want to raise and under which regulation. Then, I'd honestly assess what degree of help you're going to need with the raise. Some of these companies are very hands-off and others are more involved. Lastly, I'd take a look at the type of companies that the platform specializes in (like retail, software, etc).

While the platform that you choose is important, it's not going to replace a good marketing strategy or well-designed campaign page. In the next chapter, I'm going to do a complete brain dump on how to set up an effective equity crowdfunding campaign in a paint-by-numbers fashion. Your campaign page will be the primary mechanism that converts website visitors into investors. It's pretty freakin' important! Thankfully, if you follow these steps, you'll be able to set it up quickly, without any hassles.

Chapter 4: Making a Killer Equity Crowdfunding Campaign

Your campaign page is just about the most important asset for your offering. This is the page that's going to turn visitors into investors. Its job is to educate, persuade, and ultimately, **convert.**

You might have all of your ducks in a row. You've done all the paperwork for your offering. You've set up a sound marketing strategy. You have a few lead investors on board.

But… if you don't have a page that effectively conveys the value of your offering, it's all useless. You might get traffic, but you won't get many investors. It's a very common problem with crowdfunding campaigns as a whole.

Let's discuss the process of creating a campaign that raises funds. This is the backbone of a successful crowdfunding campaign and it contains all of the key elements that are needed to turn lurkers into investors

Your Video Will Make or Break Your Campaign

Your crowdfunding pitch video is the *first thing* that potential investors see when they come to your campaign page. It's your first impression. It's everything.

No matter how sophisticated you think investors are, they are still human beings that are driven by emotions. Most of us have very short attention spans and in the back of our mind, we're always wondering, *"Okay, so what does this mean for me?"*

Chances are that if you're not able to communicate the benefits of your offering in a 3 minute video, the website visitor isn't going to give you the chance to waste more of their time with the text below it.

My pitch video checklist reads as follows:

- **Duration:** Keep it under 5 minutes. Ideally 2 – 4. The video is a teaser. It's not meant to convey EVERYTHING about your offering.

- **Imagery to include:** Your video is all about the vision you have for the startup. It should paint a picture in the mind of a potential investor. Show the product in action. Show people using the product. Show the trustworthy team behind the offering.

- **Points to mention:** Along with the standard points, I would also throw in credibility-indicators, social proof, growth opportunity, and what investors are joining when they participate.

- **Story:** A standard pitch is going to go through the product/solution and how it's different. While you could logically discuss this it's going to be more palatable if you embed this in a story. Why were you so determined to make this solution a reality?

Investors are humans and humans are not initially moved my logic. They're moved by appeals to emotion. Suck them in with emotions and justify the offering with logic to get someone to commit to investing.

Image-Heavy Campaign Pages Win Out

The human mind is only capable of digesting a small amount of text before it gets frustrated and overwhelmed. You'll quickly lose someone's attention if your entire offering is comprised of text.

You can get around this dry or dull-looking page by including high resolution images, gifs, icons, and headlines that will break up the layout. This also will help visitors get a better sense of your company when they see more people using your product.

Don't just do this arbitrarily, but use the images on the page to draw someone's attention to a key benefit of the product or offering. It's a simple exercise in branding and storytelling.

Let's be honest, most people are gonna skim your page a couple of times before making any kind of decision. Their eyes will gravitate to the sections of the page that are easiest to read. None of us like doing a lot of work to digest information.

Effective Copywriting Will Boost Your Results

Many entrepreneurs make the mistake of thinking that the purpose of a campaign page is simply to *convey information.* Not true! The best campaign pages are very similar to sales pages. When writing a sales page, you are not only educating about the product, but you're also persuading the reader. You're getting them to take some kind of action.

Copywriting is the science of using words to persuade customers or investors to take action. You can use copywriting techniques to evoke emotions, get someone revved up, and have them invest in your offering.

Replace your BORING business speak with personable language. Remember, you're talking to retail investors, not venture capital firms. The average person is going to get bored listening to you rattle on about statistics. Try to spice it up and make it fun.

The EASIEST way that you can write more effective copy is to tell the story leading up to this moment in time and then paint the vision of the future. Why is this so effective?

- We instantly *pay attention* to good stories, because we want to find out what happens next.

- We *empathize* with main characters and the struggles they go through.

- Everyone *wishes* they were part of a good story. Now... they can be by becoming an investor.

Before anyone makes a purchasing or investment decision, they must first imagine themselves owning the actual product. In marketing terms, we call this future pacing. By painting a picture of what the future will look like, you'll get them to imagine it themselves.

The more we tend to think about something in a positive light, the greater we come to *want* that thing. Eventually, that leads to action.

For example, let's pretend that you just met an *attractive girl or guy* on the street. Without realizing it, you bumped into them while walking on the sidewalk. Oops!

After the initial confusion, you exchanged a few words. They seemed pretty cool (not to mention, they are good looking). Eventually, you got their contact information.

For the rest of the day, you can't stop thinking about them. You keep imagining what it would be like to take them out on a date, and where you would go. The more you think about them that week, the more you imagine other scenarios, like getting married or what kind of life they lead.

When you're young, it's pretty common to feel this way about someone else, and it's called *having a crush.* Your imaginings cause you to actually like them more.

The same principle applies to marketing. The more you can get potential investors to think about your company in a positive light and wonder about the future, the more they will fall in love with your team, your product, and the opportunity.

Ground Your Pitch in Reality With Numbers

In the beginning of this section, we mainly discussed ways to *evoke emotions* in your potential investors. This is extremely important, because everyone makes decisions based on emotions. However, they then justify those decisions based on logic.

If you don't have a strong appeal to the logical side of the brain in your pitch, then you're not going to close many people in the funding round. People might get all excited, but they won't take action for fear of making a **bad decision.**

To get investors to take action, you gotta give them sound reasoning as to WHY this is a great investment decision. You do that with:

- **Numbers:** How much money are you making? How many users do you have? Numbers ground your pitch in reality.

- **Statistics and Research:** How does the overall industry stack up? What do independent firms say about the niche, technology, or market? What about customer behavior?

- **Percentages and graphs:** How fast are you growing month over month? What is your retention rate?

- **Case Studies:** What are your real success stories? Who demonstrates and makes the story more concrete?

These are some easy ways to add more credibility to your pitch and ground it in reality. Some of your investors will be more rational-minded and they'll LOVE that you have all this data.

Honestly? Other investors won't care as much, but they will still like to see it because it confirms that they are making a good decision. You've clearly done your homework.

Eventually, investors will only be able to evaluate the opportunity based on the numbers you give them in the form of the minimum required investment and the shares they're getting for that.

Your Team is The Only Thing That Matters

Newer investors are more likely to believe that success in the startup space comes down to "having a good idea" or a "good market" to go after. Not true!

Of course, you need an amazing product, but if you really think about how that product comes into existence, it's because a team gets together and creates it.

We can talk strategy all day, but when it comes down to it, your startup team is actually what's going to execute on the plan. A company is just a team of people that are organized and working towards a common goal.

A great team is:

- **Talented:** The quality of the product you create is directly tied to the skill level of the team members. The more talented the team, the better the quality of product and thus the overall organization.

- **Hungry:** You can have talented people, but if they aren't hungry, they are pretty useless. Startups require long hours every single week. You gotta have a team that is hungry and obsessed with the result, just like an olympic athlete.

- **Resourceful:** You're going to run into problems. You aren't always going to have the ideal amount of funding. You need people who can solve problems and be resourceful/creative.

- **Cohesive:** Lastly, you can have a few all stars on your team, but if they don't work well together, then their usefulness will cancel each other out. You need complimentary skill sets and people that can actually work together.

Experienced investors are far more likely to pay attention to the quality of your team in the early stages of a company (rather than the idea or market). In *later* funding stages, more emphasis will be given to the product-market traction and overall growth potential.

With your crowdfunding campaign page, it's your job to illustrate why your team is uniquely able to tackle this problem and provide a world-class solution. This will help people *believe* you can actually achieve what you set out to do.

Equity Crowdfunding Page Checklist

While we could talk all day about the design of a campaign page and the various elements that are going to cause someone to make an investment commitment, I want to give you a quick and actionable list of items that you can use to get together an effective page.

The checklist below is not exhaustive but it will put you on the right path for getting started with your project page. I know there's a lot of information to consume and things to do leading up to the launch of your offering. I hope this list helps to make all that easier!

Before you launch, you'll need:

1. Crowdfunding Pitch Video

2. Problem/Product/Solution. USP (Unique selling prop)

3. The Team

4. Your Company Story

5. Business Model/Growth Engine

6. Vision For The Future

7. Statistics/Market Research and Potential

8. Case Studies/Product-Market Traction

9. Offering Details

10. How You'll Use Funding/Exit Strategy

Listing all of that out, I don't want to give you the wrong idea. Remember, your campaign functions as a **SALES PITCH.** Not everyone is going to read every word. Some investors will scan to the statistics/market section and others will be more interested in your vision for the future.

You should also form an elevator pitch that you can use to succinctly communicate what your startup is about and why people should care. This can be used when you're doing podcast interviews or other media appearances. It's also great for networking.

Always keep in mind the rules that you must abide by with your offering. You should always be 100% accurate, truthful, and transparent.

Chapter 5: Marketing Your Offering and Getting Investors

Many startups and ecommerce businesses are taking advantage of the benefits that online crowdfunding has to offer, even making it their first choice over traditional methods. However, launching an equity crowdfunding campaign can be a bit trickier than launching on a rewards-based crowdfunding platform, like Indiegogo or Kickstarter.

For one, the risk for investors is higher, and usually, so is the amount they are investing. Rather than putting $25 or $50 into a campaign, an investor is putting in $1,000 - $10,000. This means that you, as the marketer, need to do more convincing page visitors of the value of the investment. Your investors will be expecting a *future payout*, not just the ability to own the first version of the product.

"Equity crowdfunding brings both the capital and the crowd but along with that potential huge upsides," explains Sang Lee, CEO and Founder of Return on Change, "Investors are not only your funders, but also marketers and potential consumers. An increasingly powerful and sustainable model, it's something that startups should definitely look toward."

Given all the confusion, I decided to put together a few essential tips for crafting a killer equity crowdfunding campaign. If you follow the steps I'm about to outline, you will raise more money from the crowd. Not only are these strategies proven to work, but they are also used by almost all of the majorly successful equity crowdfunding campaigns.

Keep in mind that your ability to solicit your offering will vary depending on which set of regulations you raise money under.

Build Your Following BEFORE You Launch

I can't stress how important this is. You need to bring the crowd to your equity crowdfunding campaign.

You should have:

- Active social media profiles
- Consistent content marketing (social media posts)
- A responsive email list
- Direct relationships with your core tribe.

Just because you think you have "an amazing investment opportunity" or "the next Facebook," doesn't mean that other people see your vision as clearly. Your job as an entrepreneur is to communicate your vision to the world, get buy in, and persuade the hearts and minds of people in your community.

Along with building up your own following, which can consist of customers, supporters, advisors, and investors, you should also be identifying other people who have followings that you can access.

To give you an example, the Elio Motors campaign, which raised $17 million in funding on StartEngine, was very active about getting their story into the media. They reached out to YouTubers and influencers and worked to access new pools of investors. The marketing team actually came on my podcast and shared their outreach strategy.

Basically, you should aim to have a good percentage of your funding "in the bag" as they say. These are commitments or indicators of interest from a core group of your following. An easy way to jumpstart the fundraising process is to get a commitment from a strong lead investor who not only contributes substantial capital but also brings credibility to your offering.

Your Email List is King

Your email list is the ***Holy Grail*** of all of your marketing activity. Everything that I mention in this chapter should be used to build your email list leading up to the launch of your equity crowdfunding campaign. Why is email so important? According to Mckinsey & Company, "Email conversion rates are three times higher than social media, with a 17% higher value in the conversion."

The individuals who sign up for your email list are not simply numbers. They're not just random people around the world that make up an abstract statistic. They are real human beings with thoughts, feelings, desires, and emotions. In business terms, they are **leads.**

Despite the rise of social media platforms like Pinterest, Instagram, Snapchat, Facebook, and Twitter, email is still the #1 marketing channel out there for getting regular and new investors to take action. Think of email as the "home-base" where most investors receive information about the topics that they care about.

Tomorrow, Facebook could change their algorithm so that no one sees your posts. Your website could be hacked. You could find that your Instagram profile is banned for some reason. But, you'll always have your email list. If you have 1,000 people subscribed to your email list, then 1,000 individuals have raised their hand saying, "I want to receive messages from your company." Think of a room with 1,000 people in it. That would be a massive crowd!

The reason that email is so powerful is because it allows you to direct traffic to a ***designated place*** at a ***specific*** time. You don't have to wait for people to see your messages on social media, which might be drowned out by all their other social media messages. Instead, they can all check out your crowdfunding campaign at the same time and invest in it! This is why many campaigns see so much activity and so much funding during the first day of their launch, which usually spills over into the next two days.

From the time that someone gets on your email list to the second you launch, you are building and strengthening your relationship with that person

You can't expect to just convert a cold email list into sales. You must first warm them up to the product, who you are, and why they should care. If you're an advanced marketer, I would recommend segmenting your email list to get the most out of your subscribers. You could announce your campaign first to the subscribers that are most likely to become backers, and then to the rest of your subscribers to capitalize on the social proof created with the initial core group of subscribers.

The Power of Social Media Marketing

I can already see the collective eye roll. You're a creative type, or an entrepreneur! You don't want to deal with social media. Shouldn't people just follow you, because you're awesome? Believe me, by investing some time and learning how to build up followers on your social media accounts, you'll increase your future success exponentially. When you launch an equity crowdfunding campaign, you'll have a bunch of interested individuals with whom you can share your new campaign!

If you are a *skeptic*, listen up. At the end of the day, social media should be used for one thing... to build a list of leads. You can do this by driving your social media followers to an email list. This list of leads are people who have expressed interest in you or your startup. As I've mentioned before, email is the best way to convert followers into committed investors.

I define the main social media networks as:

- **Facebook.** Facebook is one of the largest social media networks out there with 1.71 billion monthly active users in 2016. Key trends are mobile adoption, video consumption on Facebook, and the changing Facebook algorithm.

- **LinkedIn.** LinkedIn is the largest professional social network with 450 million members. The platform has grown a lot in the last few years, with the introduction of articles and content on the website.

- **Instagram.** While I don't think Instagram is as mature as Facebook with paid marketing tools, it's still a very powerful network to gain followers and get people interested in your cause.

- **Twitter.** Finally, many have argued that Twitter is a waning social network, but I don't agree. There are still a large number of people who get their news from Twitter and check it daily.

You could also look into networks like SnapChat and Pinterest, but I wouldn't include these in the main list. Ultimately, you'll probably narrow in on one or two of these social networks in the long-run. My Twitter is certainly much stronger than my Instagram. You'll find the network that is the best fit for your organization, but you should have a presence on all of them!

Now that we've outlined most of the major networks, you're probably wondering...how are you actually going to get followers? How are you going to get people to take time out of their day to follow you and receive messages related to your company?

You won't be using social media to share thoughts like "My cat just rolled over." You will be using social media as a tool to figure out what type of content your audience likes and what causes they care about.

As a rudimentary example, let's say you are trying to start a business that sells a cool new product for people into health and fitness. You decided to share a post on Facebook of a before and after photo that was sent in by a customer. Maybe it also has an inspirational caption. You also link to your crowdfunding campaign. Now, if this photo got lots of clicks and shares, that tells you that potential backers are moved by images like these. You should share more inspirational images in the future.

You may even consider creating similar content on your company's blog. In the long-term, it would attract readers to the blog, who are also part of your customer base. You will then have the opportunity to ask them to invest in your upcoming crowdfunding campaign.

Basically, there are two words that sum up why people will follow you: content marketing.

You're going to be putting out content that will either be informative/useful or entertaining. This could be content that you create or content that you find on the web. Informative content could take the form of articles, tips, ideas, and advice that you share to help them achieve their goals in some way. Entertaining content could take the form of quotes, images, shocking or inspiring facts, etc. This type of content is emotional. People will follow you based on how they perceive you will make them feel in the future. You may make them feel inspired, motivated, or hungry to reach their goals.

By continually putting out free content that resonates, you'll begin to build an audience on these different social media platforms. Yes, this takes time. Accumulating followers and improving audience engagement doesn't happen overnight. If you're just getting started, plan for this to be an eight month to a year-long process before you begin getting some momentum. In that span of time, you will figure out what types of content works best for your audience, when the best time to post is, which social media channels are a good fit for your company, and you will gain an in-depth understanding of the problems that your customers care about.

Eventually, you'll start to mix in your own "call to action" messages on social media, like asking people to invest in your crowdfunding campaign. But, you shouldn't start here. The primary focus should be to get people to follow your social media profile, so that they'll get notified when more content comes out.

After hearing this strategy, you might be thinking, "This sounds like a lot of work. How am I going to find time to do all of this?"

I've used this simple strategy to build up thousands of followers on Instagram, Facebook, and Twitter. I agree, it does get difficult to keep up with all that work! That's why I've automated most of my social media marketing. You can use a tool like one of the ones I'll mention towards the end of the chapter.

Hook Journalists and Reporters With YOUR Story

Believe it or not, but you can get the media to send free traffic to your equity crowdfunding campaign. This is why I love PR and media outreach. When a journalist decides to write about you, you'll not only gain credibility in the eyes of your backers, but you'll also gain access to all of the readers that love and trust that media publication. This entire process might seem mysterious, but journalists are just like you and me. They are busy creating value for their customers, which are readers and advertisers. They can be influenced to write about certain topics, if it will bring in more traffic and advertising dollars.

I know that you might be outsourcing this part of your campaign to a marketing company or PR agency. However, I do think it pays to know a bit about the process. That way, you can oversee their work and make sure they're not pulling a fast one on ya. Many entrepreneurs will also take the task of PR outreach on themselves.

Basically, there are two ways main to influence a journalist. You can either get their attention with a press release or direct outreach. Most entrepreneurs have never written a press release, so I'm first going to cover what to include in a press release and how to craft a compelling story. Then, I'll talk about direct outreach and go through some of the techniques I've discovered to get the media to write about you.

The first thing that you must take into account when drafting a press release for your crowdfunding campaign, is that crowdfunding differs from many other traditional product launches. There are a few elements that every campaign has in common, which I'll break down below.

Fundraising Duration: Every offering has a set fundraising duration, which will impact the amount of time that you have to take advantage of any PR attention or media hits. Therefore, you need to be super organized when drafting a PR outreach strategy. Some media publications will offer the "embargo" option if they like your project and want to write about it. Basically, this means that they will hold off on the publication of the article until a certain date.

Rewards and Perks: The rewards and perks offered throughout a crowdfunding campaign are a great way to incentivize lurkers to become investors. Some of your investors might care about the mission of your project. Some might connect with you, or find your video engaging. A good number will believe in the financial future of the project and want to get a good ROI. Others will simply want to learn about what kinds of perks you're offering. Make sure to include these in your press release. Also, by underscoring the "limited" or "scarce" nature of your perks, you'll get more people to check out your campaign.

Social Proof: Backers are more skeptical than ever! Unfortunately, a growing number of campaigns have defrauded backers or have simply not fulfilled on their promises. Therefore, any way that you can add social proof or credibility to the campaign will make it more likely that journalists will check out the project or that potential backers will. Social proof can include the number of social shares, backers, comments, or dollars given. Credibility can include media mentions, partner organizations, or simply a compelling founder story.

In addition to these elements, there are a few other items that you should keep in mind when creating the PR draft for the launch of your crowdfunding campaign.

Do you have an eye-catching headline? In the same way that click-bait news headlines give readers a reason to click through to the story, you want to have an interesting headline for your press release and the subject of your email so that a journalist has a reason to read further.

Have you included images or multimedia? Words are one way to tell a story. Images and video are other ways to get a story across very quickly in this social media driven and attention-starved world. Make sure you have high resolution images on hand that the journalist or blogger can use in their article. Often times, the number of images or multimedia you can send is limited, so provide a link where they can find more multimedia assets.

Are there quotes from the founder or team? Have you ever noticed how news or human-interest stories tend to include quotes from reputable sources? They might even quote the founder themselves, if it's a new startup company. Rather than making the journalist call you up for an interesting quote, include that quote in your press release! You can also include testimonials from backers or partners to add to the social proof of the pitch.

Is it easy to find relevant links and contact information? I can't tell you the number of times that I've been emailed asking to cover a story and the email didn't have a link to the company's website or the URL of where I can find the campaign. Make it as easy as possible for journalists to find where your campaign exists online. They might be on their mobile phone and not want to search around to find it.

Have you answered the who, what, when, where, why and how? It's true that the press release should spin an enthralling story and make the journalist envision how awesome of a story this would make for their readers. However, it also needs to include concrete facts, like when the campaign will end (or start), what the product is, who designed it, and why they are so passionate about this project.

How hard is it to read the press release? It's always best to put yourself in the shoes of someone reading the press release. Is the information easily digestible? Are the paragraphs short and to the point? Are you using active verbs and strong grammar? One easy way to get an idea of how well it's written is to read it out loud! You'll quickly catch any grammar or spelling errors. You'll also get an idea of how the sentences flow.

What emotions do you arouse in the reader? Finally, a press release is part art and part science. Ask a friend who is familiar with your industry to read your press release and analyze how they feel after having read the story behind the crowdfunding effort. Are they excited to learn more? Bored? Are they confused? Simple questions like these will give you an idea of the tweaks you might need to make to elicit the desired emotional response.

You can also get journalists interested in your press release by fitting your story into the overall media environment. Identify how your crowdfunding campaign relates to hot topics and trends that journalists and bloggers are currently writing about. For example, right now, teaching coding in inner-city schools is gaining traction. There are niche blogs writing about programming, education, and STEM. There are also larger publications creating content about the technology industry.

If you created a crowdfunding campaign to help educate kids about coding, you may want to consider contacting publications that have written about these topics, as you are a prime example of a growing trend and therefore newsworthy.

Again, how does your story fit into the overall global discussion? What trends are you a part of? Research the publications engaged in these trends.

The other thing that I'll say before I share how to go about contacting journalists is that you must appeal to multiple audiences. Is your startup a new tech product that will have a big impact on a particular industry? What organizations will benefit down the road if your campaign raises the needed funds?

For example, when Arnold Schwarzenegger was working to attract media attention for his breakout film Conan the Barbarian, he appealed to multiple audiences in order to get the ink needed to fill theaters.

"To promote the movie, it was important to work every possible angle. We used special-interest magazines to build an audience – stories on sword fighting for the martial-arts magazines. Stories for horse magazines. Stories for swords and sorcery. Stories for bodybuilding magazines on how you needed top conditioning to be Conan." – Total Recall: My Unbelievably True Life Story

Let's start to talk about how you can directly contact journalists and get them to write about your crowdfunding campaign. Email is still the preferred method of contact, but I've also seen campaigners get media stories by contacting journalists via Twitter and LinkedIn.

How do you stand out from the crowd? According to a survey conducted by BuzzSumo, Journalists receive 25-100 pitches via email per day and countless more on social media. In order to stand out, it's best to avoid cliché buzzwords and stick to a succinct, straight-forward, and relevant pitch

Be succinct. Get to the point, and if needed, use bullet-points to highlight the major reasons why this news is important and a good fit for the publication. Don't write an essay. Your email should be scannable.

Be straight-forward. Avoid PR buzzwords that only serve to make it more difficult to understand your story and why it's a good fit for the publication. Otherwise, you will sound like all the other companies pitching the journalist and fail to stand out.

Be relevant. Why this journalist, why your company, and why does this story matter now? Don't just copy and paste generic emails. Tailor your pitch to both the reporter and the publication.

When is the best time to pitch a reporter? After conducting several informal interviews, PrDaily put together an awesome breakdown of the best time(s) to reach out to a journalist. Overwhelmingly, all of the reporters surveyed preferred to be pitched via email in the early morning. However, due to the large volume of weekend mail, the participants also suggested to wait until Tuesday, once the Monday rush was over and they had more time to look over each email.

This information is corroborated by MarketConsensus, who also recommended sending pitch emails between 8 am – 11 am and to avoid Mondays.

Should you send mass emails and if so, when? Despite the overwhelming industry advice not to send mass emails, I've actually seen responses from them and I've gotten stories as a result of them. Many journalists may not like these practices, but they can work if you have a killer headline, pitch, and are going after a bunch of publications with a similar audience.

However, I do think they should be used in conjunction with direct pitching and relationship building. That being said, if you're going to send out a mass email with services like PRWeb, MyPrGenie, PRNewswire, SBWire, or others, then take into account the best time to send that email. Subscribers' top engagement times are 8 a.m. – 10 a.m. and 3 p.m. – 4 p.m. with up to 6.8% average open rates and CTR (click through rate).

PR goes to experts in their space Sometimes when you're marketing a new fundraising effort, it's easy to forget that you're in "this" for the long haul, whether that's growing your company or starting a new one.

In my experience, experts in their space will never have to worry about getting PR. What was the first thing that happened on TV when Malaysia Airlines Flight 370 disappeared? The media brought aviation experts on to comment about the event and the implications.

Experts are cited in the media all the time! Even I was quoted in a recent CNN interview. The important thing is to put yourself out there as an expert, so that you can seize these opportunities for some free PR. How can you frame yourself as an expert in your space and use that as an angle for a story, or to get some free PR indirectly? HARO is a great free resource for these types of PR hits.

87% of Reporters love data, facts, and figures. Have you ever noticed when a "new study" is released that analyzes data points to corroborate or highlight an interesting trend, it goes viral on news outlets? How can you enhance your pitch with facts, figures, and data? How does your company fit into a larger cultural trend?

Backing up your vision and story with numbers is a great way to snag attention away from other pitchers, just pushing their "game changing" initiative.

P.S. Just kidding about the 87%

Journalists must write about things they don't want to. I'll tell you a little secret. Journalists don't necessarily want to write about every story, but sometimes they have to.

You're really going to tell me that if a holiday is coming around, like Christmas, that a publication isn't going to look for Christmas stories? Or if a particular story is blowing up like the Potato Salad

Kickstarter, an editor isn't going to say "I want this story on my desk by ____."

Newspapers are in the business of attracting eyeballs and advertisement dollars. Most major publications always need to write about what is trending, or they'll be left out of the flow of online and mobile traffic.

The question is: How can you fit yourself into the stories that are trending. You need to begin to think about what kinds of stories reporters will be looking for given the time of the year and what's happening in the current media discussion.

Repeat business = success. There is a big difference between a startup that repeat customers and one-time customers. The same is true for PR. Rather than seeking one-time transactional relationships, it's best to develop a long-term relationship with a journalist. They may move publications in the future, and you'll be able to continue to get PR hits. They might also forward you along to his or her friends, who are also journalists.

You should take a long-term view of PR outreach. This is exactly what a PR agency does, and they are in the business of getting their clients stories. Why wouldn't you take the same approach as a professional PR firm?

A relationship with even a handful of reporters can yield dividends down the road. Go out of your way to be helpful to them. Connect them with sources or people in your industry they'd like to speak with.

Your email headline must be clickable. It's hard to have a clickable headline without knowing your audience, which brings us back to point #1 (relevancy). Ideally, your headline should be tailored to the individual reporter or publication.

Your name and headline are the first few things a reporter is going to see when they look at your email. How can you phrase the headline to get them interested in learning more?

One technique I've found to be helpful is to see if there are any headline commonalities in other articles that have been published by that reporter and then craft your email subject to be similar to those headlines.

There is no blueprint. Although there are "best practices" and mistakes to avoid, getting PR is a learning process. You need to figure out what works well for your company and your industry, which will take time.

Personally, I've had experiences that fly in the face of the common industry advice in terms of the ideal times to send emails and how to best do journalist outreach. Keep in mind that these are general guidelines, and they are not set in stone.

I think the most worthwhile takeaway you should get from this section is that you need to adopt a PR mindset. You need to begin to observe the news, TV, and print media and begin to form questions. Why did a publication quote this expert, or why did this reporter choose to write about this particular story? Beginning to make yourself aware of the inner-workings of the news media will help you begin to become active on the pitching side.

These key rules form the bedrock of a sound marketing strategy. You should always have them at the back of your mind when you're engaged in backer communications. They're used every day by marketers to sell products to the public. They aren't just for businesses though. You can steal them and apply these techniques to getting visitors to take action and invest in your offering. They're proven to influence the only thing that matters, getting your backers to *take action*.

Make sure that you are connected via phone, email and on social media. Keep your followers up-to-date with your progress.

Celebrate milestones. Share news. Get them to participate in the upcoming campaign! Having an initial surge of investors at the beginning of a project encourages others to invest.

Masterful Caveman Storytelling Secrets

It's pretty rare that a product or project is so innovative that its existence is genuine *news.*

By news I mean that when you're telling someone that "this product now exists," their eyes would go wide and they say *"no way!"*

Journalists are certainly looking to cover informational news announcements, but they are also looking for *stories* that their readers would like.

This can be your secret weapon!

When you craft a compelling story, you'll instantly get the attention of a reader. They'll go through the article, wondering what's going to happen next. As they read, they'll come to have thoughts, opinions, and even experience a change in their perspective.

You can embed a product announcement *WITHIN* a story. When done right, the story will also generate more positive feelings towards the product or the team that created it.

These are the basic elements of a story:

- Main character with values and a world view.

- An event that happens that causes the start of a journey.

- Main character who has a goal.

- Conflict or opposing forces that prevent that goal from being achieved.

- Realizations or victories.

- Insights or defeats.

- Ultimate conclusion.

The craft of storytelling has existed for thousands of years. You can COPY everything that works when it comes to engaging an audience, keeping their interest, and moving them towards a climax.

I'm not saying that you have to use EVERY technique that I'm going to reveal when it comes to sharing your company's story with the world. However, if you incorporate one or two, it will dramatically boost the emotional appeal of your offering.

Personally, I have used the exact same tips to write stories emotionally affect my audience. You can use them to improve your writing, sell more creative work, or get your message across in an emotionally evocative way.

The first key part of storytelling is that every story has a conflict. I hate the word "conflict." It sounds like bullshit literary jargon.

You can sum conflict up like this:

1. Your main character has something they want.

2. They try to get it or achieve it.

3. Things stop them from doing that.

First, your main character must have **something they want.** Your side characters likely have things they want as well. If your main character does not want something, then there is no story.

Your main character could want multiple things, but there is one overarching desire that they have that guides all of their behavior.

For example, James Bond wants to defeat the arch enemy or villain in the movie.

Simba from the Lion King wants to realize his destiny and become king.

Marlin in Finding Nemo wants to find his son.

Frodo in Lord of the Rings wants to destroy the ring.

The "desires" or "wants" of the main characters can be so obvious that the entire movie is named after them, like "The Lion King" or "Finding Nemo."

Second, your main character attempts to get, achieve, or *fulfill this desire* in some way. Usually, this is sort of "kicked off" with the inciting incident or plot turning points. The main character doesn't necessarily always realize they have this desire in them to begin with.

For example, with Lord of the Rings, Frodo only gets his desire to destroy the ring once it is entrusted to him and he understands the bad things that could happen if he doesn't.

Up until this point in time, he was just another Hobbit in the shire living out his life. Of course, he always did love hearing about the adventures of Gandalf or Bilbo.

In Finding Nemo, Marlin always had the desire to protect and take care of his son, but he only gained the desire to "find" his son when he got lost and was taken away.

Once that happens, Marlin goes on a quest to try to find his son and get him back.

Third, for some reason your main character does not immediately achieve their objective. There is **conflict.** They are prevented from achieving it for some reason. This is a crucial part of storytelling. If Frodo just walked down the path to Mordor and easily destroyed the ring, then there would be no story. There must be forces of opposition.

There are a lot of things that could prevent the main character from achieving their objective. That could include:

- Other characters (with opposing interests)
- Themselves (their nature, beliefs, thoughts)
- Society
- Nature, etc.

The main character is continually met with forces of opposition as they are trying to achieve their goal. Over time, this causes the character to GROW.

In the beginning of the Lion King, Simba is not yet ready to be king. He must grow physically and emotionally until he can become strong enough to defeat Scar and accomplish his goal.

At one point, Simba had opposition within himself. He had lost his way and didn't care about being King. He was just living in the jungle having a good time.

Remember, "hakuna matata." It means "no worries!"

It was only when he was reminded about things he cared about and what was at stake, that he decided to come back and challenge Scar.

Continual conflict is what makes an audience interested in finding out "what happens next." It peaks curiosity, and as the audience gets to know the characters, creates emotional investment.

It's one of the elements at play behind the marketing genius, **Steve Jobs** and why he always pitted his technology startup against large entrenched competitors, like IBM.

But, conflict is not enough. It might get you attention, but it doesn't make people care about the outcome. A story only matters because it has stakes. This is another one of those literary terms that I don't like.

When something has "stakes" it really means that something is "at stake." There are things that will be lost UNLESS the objective is achieved. There is a clear and obvious downside if the main character fails.

In a classic Superman storyline, if he fails to defeat Lex Luther or whatever other villain, then the world will fall into chaos. The villain will take over, make things bad for everyone else, ruin good values, and get what he wants (which are bad things).

Throughout a story, the more stakes that there are, the more the audience's attention will be drawn to find out "what happens next." Will Superman defeat the villain, or will he die, lose Lois Lane, fail his mother, and submit the world to the rule of a horrible leader.

As you can see, not only are there things (internally and externally) that seek to prevent the main character from achieving his objective, but there are also downsides should the main character fail.

If a story had zero stakes, then it wouldn't be worth paying attention to.

Let's just say that in the Lord of the Rings example, the one ring actually didn't have any real powers. It was just a "symbol" of previous bad times.

Frodo tries to destroy it, because it's a symbol, and the Orcs don't want it destroyed, because it's a symbol. But, since there's no real power and nothing really bad can come of it's existence, you're left thinking... "well, what's the point?"

The fact that the ring can cause real damage and unleash evil is what causes Frodo to care about the quest and embark upon it.

You can apply this to YOUR startup's offering by underscoring what's at risk if you don't succeed. You can rally others around your startup's central purpose.

However, even if you have conflict built into your founding story and a reason why you're pursuing this mission, it doesn't mean that it will generate continual interest through your campaign or your startup's lifecycle. Thankfully, this is one secret for maintaining the interest and attention of your investors. That takes the form of events, revelations, and decisions. In their eyes, this is what is "moving the story forward." It's why they continue to pay attention.

Put simply, stories are "moved along" by events that occur, revelations of new information, and decisions that must be made. As the story gets more intense, the pressure goes up and forcing characters to make big decisions. Ultimately, true character is revealed when these decisions are made.

First, let's talk about events that occur. These events could be things that happen to the main character, events that happen in the world, or reactions to things the characters are doing. These events prompt characters to make decisions or change attitudes.

I know that initially, this might not seem to make sense in the context of startup investing but stay with me.

When Frodo is unable to find Gandalf in the Prancing Pony and accidentally puts on the ring, which attracts forces of evil, he must make the decision to trust Aragon and follow him to safety.

New information is also always coming to light, which the characters then react to. **Withholding information** is a major way to maintain curiosity throughout a story.

How boring would it be if we knew ALL ALONG that Darth Vader was Luke Skywalker's father?

Instead, in that moment of revelation, we gain tremendous clarity about past events. Luke must then make the decision whether or not to join his father, who is on the dark side, or to continue with the resistance movement.

This decision reveals his character. If he said "yes" and joined his father, we'd think differently about him. Up until that point in the film, we thought he was one of the good guys.

We'd be confused and secretly wonder if he was going to try to fight the empire from the inside out, or if his sister would pick up the mantel. All of these events/revelations trace back to what's at "stake" and the "motivation" of the characters, otherwise they wouldn't have meaning.

For example, let's just say Star Wars started with the scene of Luke discovering Darth Vader was his father. You didn't know any of the backstory.

We'd be left thinking... "Wow, Luke looks really upset. I wonder why?"

We'd then expect the rest of the story to fill in the gaps. That moment wouldn't have much significant until that happened. Instead, because we KNOW that:

- Luke is trying to destroy the evil empire and restore good

- If Luke doesn't do this (as the last jedi), the rebel forces might perish and evil would exist forever unchallenged

- Luke has no father and his adopted parents were killed by storm troopers

When we watch the same scene, we think "oh my gosh!" Luke has been fighting his entire adult life trying to combat evil, and all the while it's been his father that has been opposing him.

Also, the mysterious backstory starts to make more sense. We now know why his mentor hid many of the facts about his father (who he said Vader murdered).

It's a realization that his mentor was lying in order to keep him from knowing the terrible truth. It gives the feeling that the "world is crashing down" around Luke. Then, Vader offers him to "join him and rule together."

At that moment in time, everyone is wondering... "What is Luke going to do?"

Using this example, you can easily see how this story structure of events, withholding information, and "reactions," is what moves stories along and maintains the interest of the audience.

You can ***withhold information and announcements*** that you slowly release throughout the duration of your equity crowdfunding offering. Of course, it can't be related to the financials of the company or anything like that, but it could include things like new content that is being released or influencers that you've now partnered with.

This creates the feeling that your investors are experiencing an event that's currently unfolding, making them much more attuned to your future messages. They'll want to follow along to see what happens next.

These are a few simply ways that you can bake storytelling into your marketing. I'm not saying that you have to use all of these strategies or tactics. Just pick or two. From a biological standpoint, human beings are wired to listen to and pay attention to stories. Why not use that to your advantage?

The Popularity of Paid Advertising

Paid advertising has become an extremely popular way to drive traffic to both equity crowdfunding campaigns and fundraisers on websites like Kickstarter and Indiegogo.

This advertising could be used to build up a list of email leads, spread brand awareness, or get people onto your campaign page.

Typically, it's doing through Facebook ads, Google ads, influencer marketing, or email blasts.

I'm going to go through some of the proven strategies for running profitable Facebook ads. These tips are best used for product-centric campaigns.

At the same time, as we saw with the last election, you can also use Facebook ads to get people to take action in a number of different industries, whether it's for a cause-related, political, or nonprofit crowdfunding campaign.

There are a few different variables when it comes to Facebook advertisements. There is:

- **The creative.** This is the image that you use to convey your message on the platform.

- **The copywriting.** This is also part of the message that users see. It should persuade them of the value of clicking on the advertisement.

- **The audience.** Who is going to see this advertisement and how are they connected to you. Are they cold leads or warm leads?

- **The offer.** This is the value you're offering users. This is the overall reason they should click on your advertisement.

In the points below, I'm going to be hitting on several of these variables and how you can employ a strategy to get the most bang for your buck.

Custom Audience: I've found that advertising to a custom audience tends to be the greatest ROI for my ad spend. This could take the form of website visitors or a look-a-like audience, but I'll get into that later.

At the moment, I'm referring to the option where you can upload a **list of email subscribers** and Facebook will advertise to those individuals on their platform. You might say to yourself... why would I want to do that when I could just send them an email?

Good question!

The reason is that not everyone is going to open your emails. Depending on the size of your email list, you could be getting anywhere from 20 – 50% open rates. This will also vary depending on how receptive people are to you and your message.

If you have an email list of 2,000 people, that could be 400 – 1,000 people who are not receiving your messages! You could create a custom email list of people who are not opening your emails and upload it to Facebook. You could also just upload the entire list.

The great thing about this approach is that individuals who have signed up to your email list are pre-selected to be interested in your offer. They've already taken the time to give you their email address.

This is why you're going to tend to see more of a profitable ad spend when you create a custom audience in this manner. People already:

- Know who you are.

- Are interested in what you have to offer.

There are a lot of different types of email lists that you can upload, including:

- A list of blog subscribers

- A pre-launch list

- A list of previous customers

They're warm leads.

Retargeting Ads: Now that you've uploaded a list of leads that you've generated from your marketing, it's time to take your Facebook advertising a step further.

Another way that you can create a custom audience in Facebook is with your own website traffic. You can target people who have come to your website in the past.

Since SO MANY people use Facebook (1.15 billion mobile daily active users), it's likely that they're also going to be on Facebook. You might have visited a website or looked into a particular product and then noticed that you started to get ads on that product in your Facebook feed. This is the power of retargeting ads.

Of course, if you want to do this, you're going to need to install a Facebook pixel on your website. You gotta let it collect data for a little bit, then you'll be ready to go!

When you create a custom audience of people who have visited your website, I'd recommend identifying key pages that segment your website audience.

For example, let's say that you have a page on your website with information about your upcoming equity crowdfunding campaign. Awesome!

Anyone who visits this page is clearly interested in learning more about your product, so this would be a great audience to re-target.

Now, let's say that you wrote a blog post that's not related to your product, but instead shares some of your own thoughts at this stage in your life. This would NOT be a good page to retarget website traffic from. It's not relevant to your current product offering.

Similar to drawing from your pre-existing email lists, retargeting ads have a few different benefits:

- People already know you or your company, as they visited your website.

- People have a vague idea of what you're offering.

- People have qualified themselves as being semi-warm leads, meaning that they're more likely to convert into backers than cold leads.

These are the key reasons why retargeting ads tend to be low hanging fruit. They're a profitable way to begin to get more crowdfunding campaign backers.

Lookalike Audience: A third way that you can begin to get more backers for your crowdfunding campaign using Facebook ads is to take advantage of lookalike audiences.

Here's how it works. Facebook will create a list of users that have similar attributes to those that you've designated. They use their proprietary algorithm to do this. This algorithm has gotten pretty good over the years.

You can create a lookalike audience from:

- Your email list

- Your website traffic

- Other custom audiences you've built.

Seeing as these users will be similar to the individuals you've designated, they're going to be more likely to be interested in your offer and take action on your advertisement. This is the reason lookalike audiences tend to be more profitable.

Along with creating a lookalike audience, you can also designate other ways to narrow down the potential audience. You could preselect that people must be interested in key topics, like ecommerce, startups, or technology.

There are a lot of different variables that you can choose from to make sure this audience is highly relevant. You can even target people who follow key individuals or pages.

Up until this point in time, there were only a few variables that you could play with to affect your conversion rates. This included your image, copywriting, and overall offer.

Now, you can play with many more variables to get better conversion rates. This is both good and bad. I'd try to run one test at a time and see how it affects that results you're seeing in term of the click through rate, sign up rate, and overall engagement.

Target Cold Users: A "warm" user is someone who has already interacted with your brand in some way. A "cold" user is someone who has no idea who you are and what you're offering. They haven't expressed any kind of interest in your offer.

Lookalike audiences are a form of cold traffic that you'd be sending to your campaign. A step beyond that is to simply check the boxes of the various interests that you want to target on Facebook.

For example, if someone has expressed an interest in fashion or shopping, and you checked that box, those individuals would receive your advertisement.

This is where most beginners start, but it's the least effective way to get bakers for your crowdfunding campaign. You're really shooting into the dark and unless you have a stellar offer, you're likely going to get less of an ROI.

I would engage in this strategy last, as it's the riskiest. Still, you can always throw $10 per day at Facebook ads and test it. It's not going to break the bank.

When you have all of these four pillars of Facebook ads working successfully, you've reached the crowdfunding holy grail. You'll be able to confidently say that you can turn $1 into $4 using Facebook ads.

Marketing Tools

Getting investors interested in your equity crowdfunding offering is a lot tougher than most entrepreneurs realize.

It's not like investors are going to start pouring in once you launch and you're magically going to get funded. You have to put in the work to market the crowdfunding page, spread awareness, and get investors.

Thankfully, if you're strapped for cash, there are some tools out there to make the process MUCH easier.

Boomerang: You can use Boomerang to do a few different things, including scheduling emails to go out at a specific time, getting reminders of when you need to follow up on an email, and write emails that have the highest chance of getting a response.

Their new "respondable" feature takes into account subject length, word count, question count, reading level, positivity, politeness, and subjectivity to determine how likely it is you're going to get a reply to your email.

I think the tool is most powerful for setting reminders to follow up with specific investors, journalists, or influencers. The app will tell you if the email was not opened, if your link in the email wasn't clicked, or if you didn't get a reply.

This is a great tool when you're doing individual outreach to build relationships that could turn into investments, media hits, partners, or advisors.

Leadpages + MailChimp: This is a deadly combo for your pre-launch when you're building an email list. Leadpages is a very simple tool to set up a conversion-optimized email capture.

Of course, I recommend that you have your own domain name and website, but very often marketers will set up a unique landing page apart from their main website to test traffic conversions.

You don't want to send all of your traffic to your homepage leading up to the launch of your equity crowdfunding campaign. You want to send it to a landing page where you can measure conversions to an email list or other type of call-to-action.

LeadPages will tell you how many visitors you've sent to a particular landing page and the conversion rate to your email list. You can then A|B test landing pages or change around the wording to see how that impacts your conversion rate.

The other tool that I'd pair LeadPages with is MailChimp. MailChimp makes it super easy to manage your email list, send out newsletters, and stay connected with your subscribers. The great news is that it's also free up until 2,000 subscribers (at the time of writing).

MailChimp handles all of the list-building functionality and gives you data on open rates and conversion stats. It will also give you some cool graphs to show you how your campaigns are progressing.

To give you an example, I'll share some of the basic stats from my personal blog, where I talk about books I read, conclusions I've come to in my life, and some of my business realizations. I don't really market my personal blog at all, so it's much smaller than all of my other websites.

Email Hunter: Email Hunter is one of many apps that you can use to get the email address of the webmasters of websites that you come across.

I'm not saying that you should spam these webmasters, but if you're looking to do cold outreach or connect directly with bloggers/journalists, this can be a very useful tool.

Also, if you're trying to connect with influencers, this tool can also be useful so that you don't spend hours and hours looking for an email address.

I'm all about saving you time, money, and headache!

Buzzsumo: Going along with the theme of saving YOU time, BuzzSumo is an amazing website for finding influencers and seeing what types of media stories are trending for various topics.

I think that BuzzSumo is a great place to start when you're trying to build up an audience with content marketing, but it's also a great way to develop story angels for when you're reading out to journalists.

Not all of the information with all of these tools will be 100% accurate, which is why it's important to have a multi-tiered approach. For example, I put in the term crowdfunding and CLEARLY I should be one of the top influencers (hahah just kidding), but I'm not listed.

Angel Capital Association: While not a software tool, the Angel Capital Association is a great directory to draw from when building relationships with Angel Investors.

Keep in mind that with a Title III equity crowdfunding campaign, anyone can invest in your startup, but you'll still need bigger investors who can put larger sums into your company to make the fundraising process easier.

You can use the directory to find groups and events happening in your area.

Wistia: I use Wistia for my online courses because they're a great tool for tracking analytics on your videos and also having specific call-to-actions. Basically, it's a marketer's dream.

For example, you can use the heat-map feature to see which portions of your pitch investors are skimming over or are re-watching.

You can also set up specific call-to-actions like asking for an email address before someone views the video pitch. Don't get me wrong, I also use YouTube to share videos online, but I find that Wistia is a much better tool if you're hosting a video on your own website and are looking for more in-depth analytics.

Buffer: I've talked about Buffer a lot because it's my go-to-tool for automating my social media profiles, like my Twitter, Instagram, and Facebook.

You can use Buffer to schedule all of your social media posts ahead of time, along with getting data on who's viewing your posts, clicking on the various links, and engaging with your content.

This is very powerful because it then allows you to tailor your social media posts going forward and focus in on certain types of language or messages that are resonating with your followers.

Chapter 6: Mastering Investor Psychology

The media gives the impression that business is all about dry numbers and calculation. While analytics and data are immensely helpful, what's even more useful for boosting your sales is actually quite rare. It's empathy, plain and simple. The more that you can empathize with the emotions that your target customers are feeling, the better. You can then amplify the emotions that lead to buying your product or backing your campaign.

In this chapter, we'll discuss some ways that you can employ Jedi Mind Tricks to stand out above all the other crowdfunding campaigns out there, gain credibility, enhance the trustworthiness of your company, and get website visitors to take action!

Rule #1: Social Proof Creates Trust and Lowers Defensive Barriers

I'm a pretty normal young man living in NYC. I don't smell, I'm reasonably intelligent, and I'm told I have a nice smile.

But, if I were to go up to a random person on the street and say "Hi, nice day, right?" more often than not, I'd get looks of confusion, suspicion, annoyance, and many people would nervously smile and rush past.

I know this because I actually do this sometimes just to work on my social skills and face social fear.

People are naturally suspicious in our culture of strangers and organizations that we haven't heard of before. It's because the person **suspects** that the other person wants something from them, which puts them on the defensive and raises their guard.

There is no familiarity, trust, or value in the interaction. Also, everyone else is on their way to work or another destination, so it feels "weird" for them to respond to or stop and talk to a complete stranger. It's an interruption.

Social proof is one way to jump this barrier and gain instant trust. Here's how Wikipedia defines it:

"Social proof, also known as informational social influence, is a psychological phenomenon where people assume the actions of others in an attempt to reflect correct behavior for a given situation. This effect is prominent in ambiguous social situations where people are unable to determine the appropriate mode of behavior, and is driven by the assumption that surrounding people possess more knowledge about the situation."

When a product or individual has social proof, others will approach them from a perspective of **curiosity** rather than skepticism. They're more likely to take a second to watch your video or read your fundraising page because "other people think it's interesting, so I might as well check it out."

It's basically thinking that just because a book is bestselling that it's probably good and worth buying. You might even take less time to check it out than a non-bestselling book.

If you've ever seen a bunch of people surrounding one person in a group setting, I'm willing to bet you thought, "Is that a celebrity?" or you were more apt to go and join the crowd yourself to see who they were.

Social proof evokes curiosity. When you lead with social proof, rather than being skeptical, the prospective backer is more likely to focus on the mission, story, or awesome impact that your company has had. They'll be intrigued instead of suspicious.

There are a few ways to create social proof, including:

- Testimonials

- Genuine activity and donations

- Comments section

- Media hits/write-ups

- Social sharing

- Reviews/emails

- Credentials and endorsements

While growing vanity metrics like social media followers or the number of visitors to your website shouldn't be your main goal, they can be leveraged to enhance your credibility in the minds of potential backers. This is one way to get visitors to take action. A campaign with high social proof is more likely to convert browsers into backers. Rather than clicking off your page, a visitor is going to open their wallet and put in their credit card information.

The worst thing that could happen is that a visitor comes to your campaign and sees 0 investors, 0 social shares, and a half-baked "ask." It makes them feel like little real work went into putting together the startup page. They'll rationalize that either the company isn't serious, that the cause isn't worthy of their funds, or that something else is wrong, because no one else has given money.

On the flip side, if someone discovers your campaign online and sees a bunch of investors pouring in or massive engagement and social sharing activity, they're more likely to take a sec to watch your video and read through your pitch. The fact that other people are paying attention to the crowdfunding effort makes them want to learn more. It evokes curiosity and engenders a stronger feeling of trust.

Rule #2: A Sense of Urgency is What Prompts Action

The reason that people *take action* is because there's an impending deadline or other event, which creates a sense of urgency.

I don't know about you, but I was definitely one of those kids who procrastinated most of the college semester and then crammed two days before the exam. Many of my nights were spent in the library the day before a final paper was due.

Of course, the best and most *rational* thing to do is to plan, take action according to your plan, and see the desired result. But, most people aren't rational. We're guided by our emotions.

When someone feels a sense of urgency about a particular activity, they will:

- Focus and drone out distractions.

- Take massive action in a small amount of time.

- Overcome hurdles that would normally set them back.

- Pay less attention to hindering emotions or thoughts.

- Look to short-cut signals to make micro decisions.

- Take more risks.

I've written and spoken extensively about how a crowdfunding campaign's fundraising meter will grow and flatten out over time. Many campaigners see an influx of pledges towards the beginning and end of their campaign. Both of these events create a sense of urgency among supporters, whether it's to claim limited quantity "rewards" or get in before the doors close on your campaign.

The best marketers are able to prompt action throughout the duration of their fundraising campaign. But, the great thing about crowdfunding is that the basic model *encourages* urgency due to the temporal nature of the fundraiser. It's your job, as a campaign manager, to communicate this emotion to your backers, so that they feel this urgency. Don't just assume they'll feel it. Communicate it. Repeatedly.

The more you create a sense of urgency in the minds of your backers and campaign visitors, the better the chance that they'll actually take action and give money to your project. Of course, this is assuming that you put together a great campaign page. Even with a great page, you'll still raise money, but when you effectively communicate urgency, you'll raise even more money.

Rule #3: Build Relationships at Scale

Okay, I get A LOT of emails and many of them start like this...

"Hey Sal. Love the blog and podcast. Tell me, how do I get strangers to invest in my campaign?"

First of all, I don't give out a lot of free advice directly, because I'd be on my email all day long. I direct people to my FREE online content. I do offer consulting, mentorship, and coaching programs.

Second of all, you can't get strangers to back your campaign. However, you can turn strangers into FRIENDS and then get them to invest in your project. It's a subtle distinction.

The way you do this is by building relationships at scale.

Here's the idea summed up. Since everyone thinks *you* want something from them, break the pattern by giving them something *they* want. It has to be something they actually want and it has to add value to their life in some way.

As you begin to provide quality content, advice, or free value, the people will begin to feel like they know you. When someone watches a free video that you put together, they'll get a sense of your values, and eventually, they'll develop an emotional connection with you.

This is EXACTLY why we feel like we "know" big-name YouTubers or celebrities and are completely okay shouting out their name in public or buying something they endorse. In fact, I'd go so far as saying that we feel like we "love" certain comedians because we relate with them so much and almost consider them to be a friend.

We're willing to watch a 5 minute video created by a random person in the world if it makes us say "wow," laugh until we cry, or if it resonates with us and inspires us to be a better person. When you put out content in the form of videos, emails, social media posts, blog posts, or images that educate, inspire, or entertain, you're investing in the relationship with your potential backers and customers.

Ultimately, you're doing all of this to simply build relationships with multiple people at once. A thousand people can watch one video on your Facebook page and come away feeling like they know a bit more about you and your company. This is powerful. In the past, you'd have to directly interact one-on-one with the same number of people to create that type of response.

When you do this over a span of time, you can get 1,000 people to subscribe to your email list, or to follow you on a particular social media channel. I know it works, because I've used it to build my own email list to over 20,000 subscribers. I've used these techniques to grow an online forum to over 6,000 users, get over 100 positive iTunes reviews for my podcast, and make a living doing what I love. By the way, I'm a millennial. When I started, I didn't have what older people label as "experience." If a kid can figure this out, so can you. I'm also giving away the formula. You just have to copy it. Remember, all of this is what gives you the leverage that you need to CRUSH IT during the first week of your offering.

Rule #4: Stories Trump Logic

When is the last time that you sat through a two hour long YouTube video lecture? Probably never (though if you have, that's awesome!). But, people around the world are 100% okay with sitting through a 2 hour movie in a dark room. Even if the movie sucks, they'll stick around because they want to find out what happens.

The same goes for TV shows. How many times have we heard friends say "okay, let's just see what happens and then we'll change the channel." We'll default to this even if it's a trashy show or it isn't good, and we pretty much know what's going to happen.

Stories are powerful for three reasons:

- They create anticipation.

- They hold attention.

- They encourage empathy with the characters and challenges.

If you want someone to feel **exactly** how you felt in a given situation, weave a story around that event. Don't just tell them how you felt.

Quite simply, the best stories **communicate information** and make you **like** or at least feel close to the main character. They are a powerful vehicle for creating trust online.

Not only are they a great way to get people excited about taking action and joining your campaign's community, but they are also super good for seducing journalists and bloggers like me to write about you!

Many of the successful crowdfunding campaigners that I've had on my podcast pitched me with a compelling story, which I then wanted to share with the podcast listeners.

I hate to break it to you, but no one is going to remember the statistics you put out, not even your key customers. Statistics are an important way to establish credibility, but they aren't great for arousing strong emotions. But, I can almost guarantee you that EVERYONE will remember a compelling story. The more emotions that someone feels, the more likely they are to remember an event and also take action in the moment.

You should be sharing your story though several mediums and across multiple platforms. I'm not just talking about the social media platforms out there. I'm also referring to your email list, and when you're speaking at events.

A great story will bring listeners into your world, and when they feel what you feel, they're more likely to take the action that you think "makes complete sense." For most readers out there, that's to contribute the funds to enable a cool product or project to come to life.

Rule #5: Create the Emotion of "Liking"

Okay, I know that I sound like I'm a robot right now. I really do enjoy analyzing emotions with the rational side of my brain. I also must **strongly emphasize** that the techniques I'm sharing in this section should only be used if you genuinely believe that you have an amazing product that will make other people's lives better.

In Robert Cialdini's seminal book, Influence, he reveals 3 key points, that I'll highlight below:

- "We like people who are similar to us in terms of opinions, personality traits, background, or lifestyle."

- "Familiarity also plays a role in decisions. Seeing or experiencing something more and becoming familiar with it leads to greater liking."

- "A halo effect occurs when one positive characteristic of a person dominates the way that person is viewed by others. We assign favorable traits to good looking people without logic."

In case you missed kindergarten, when we like someone we are more likely to help them, support them, and take the time to listen to what they have to say.

I'm not saying that you should try to force people to like you or to not be genuine. I'm saying that you should be aware of the emotions that your words, imagery, video, and content creates.

Making a joke in your video might make *you* nervous, but it might make **them** laugh, feel good about themselves, and like you more.

If you're speaking to a group of programmers, you're probably going to generate a great feeling of "liking" if you yourself are also a programmer, can make inside jokes, or relate to the job lifestyle. If you're a business guy who doesn't know the first thing about programming and you assume certain things or butcher key terms, it's unlikely that the audience will see you in a favorable light.

Being focused on how much your backers like you or your team is another great way to avoid typical objections that bog down many equity crowdfunding campaigns.

For example, a skeptical backer might harp on the negative qualities of investing with regards to security of capital. Let's be honest though, this objection is a reality. This is innovation we're talking about. You then have to deal with that objection.

If that visitor likes you, then they are going to approach the campaign from an entirely different mindset. Maybe instead of focusing on *that* particular aspect, they'll smile at what you're trying to accomplish, decide to support it, and rationalize that you're a good guy so you will be forthright with issues that you or they encounter.

Of course, you should be 100% transparent and forthright with any complications. Just keep in mind that the degree to which someone likes you will affect how they rationalize the things that you ask of them.

To sum it all up, you don't come off as some faceless company with a big board of directors that is just looking to raise money. Personalize it. You want to come off as an actual human being, and in the best-case scenario, as a likeable friend.

These key rules form the bedrock of a sound marketing strategy. You should always have them at the back of your mind when you're engaged in backer communications. They're used every day by marketers to sell products to the public. They aren't just for businesses though. You can steal them and apply these techniques to getting visitors to take action and invest in your new offering. They're proven to influence the only thing that matters, getting your backers to **take action**.

Chapter 7: Investor Advice, Tips, and Strategy

Do you want to get in on the next DropBox, Uber, or Facebook?

You can now invest in startup companies online from the comfort of your own home. With the click of a button, you can become a partial owner of a new *fast-growing* tech company. You don't even need any previous experience!

Without a doubt, giving retail investors access to these previously exclusive deals is a **good thing,** but there must also be some guidance and education so that you don't lose your shirt.

Every investment comes with a certain degree of risk. This is true of the stock market, bonds, real estate, commodities, and equity crowdfunding. The riskier that something is, the higher the potential return.

With this chapter, I'm going to dive into several key equity crowdfunding tips for investors that will help you navigate this new industry.

Equity Crowdfunding Investments are Illiquid (and Profitable)

When you buy a stock on the stock market, you can immediately sell it. There is an established secondary marketplace of buyers and sellers that trade the stock.

On the one hand, this is good because it means your investment is very liquid. You can easily convert it into cash at any point in time. You don't risk "getting tied up" with one company for years on end. On the other hand, it can lead to a lot of volatility with constant trading.

"Unless you can watch your stock holding decline by 50% without becoming panic-stricken, you should not be in the stock market." – Warren Buffett

Unlike the stock market, there is no secondary market for the shares that you buy of an equity crowdfunding campaign. For the most part, you will only have an opportunity to cash out when the startup is purchased, or it goes public.

This means that you won't be able to easily convert your equity crowdfunding shares into cash. This long-term investment horizon means you'll be betting more on the fundamentals of the company.

You Have a Special Name as an Investor...

Yes YOU!

If you earn more than $200,000 per year and have more than a $1 million net worth (excluding your house), then you are referred to as an Accredited Investor.

There are some other stipulations when it comes to gaining the status of an Accredited Investor, but for the most part, it's ultra-high net worth individuals who can afford risky investments. Some institutional investors will also gain this status because of the funds they command.

Recognizing your status as an investor is important because it will determine the types of companies you can invest in and the platforms that you can use. Not every equity crowdfunding platform is created equal.

Minimums, Maximums, and Limits Imposed

Every equity crowdfunding campaign has a minimum amount that is required in order to enter the funding round. This could be $500 or $1,000. It's going to vary.

Depending on the type of investor that you are, there will also be maximums imposed as set forth in the rules for the Jobs Act and the regulation that the company is using to raise funds.

Under regulation crowdfunding, there is a limit on the amount that you can invest in a 12-month period that are outlined as follows:

- **Annual or net worth < $107,000:** You can invest up to the greater of $2,200 or 5% of your the lesser of your annual income or net worth.

- **Annual income and net worth are equal or > $107,000:** You can invest up to 10% of your income or net worth, whichever is less, but no more than $107,000.

You can find an example of this below as pulled from the SEC website.

Annual Income	Net Worth	Calculation	12-month Limit
$30,000	$105,000	greater of $2,200 or 5% of $30,000 ($1,500)	$2,200
$150,000	$80,000	greater of $2,200 or 5% of $80,000 ($4,000)	$4,000
$150,000	$107,000	10% of $107,000 ($10,000)	$10,700
$200,000	$900,000	10% of $200,000 ($20,000)	$20,000
$1.2 million	$2 million	10% of $1.2 million ($120,000), subject to cap	$107,000

These limits are imposed to help prevent investors from themselves. By having a healthy limit, it will ensure that individuals don't incur massive losses in a short amount of time. I think it's a very good idea.

Diversification Is King

Every professional investor diversifies across many different asset classes and investments. This helps spread out the risk for your portfolio.

While equity crowdfunding might fit into the "alternative finance" part of your overall diversified portfolio, I would also recommend diversifying your investments within the equity crowdfunding industry.

This means that you shouldn't put all of your eggs in one basket. Even venture capital firms will spread their checks across 10 different companies to help spread out the risk. If one firm goes belly up, it won't hurt their portfolio as long as they get one or two major wins.

Along with lowering the risk of your portfolio, diversification will also get you used to these online interfaces and get you quickly familiar with how equity crowdfunding offerings work.

Only Invest in Startups You Understand

It's very important that you ONLY invest in startup offerings that you **understand**. When you don't know what you're doing, it's a fatal mistake.

As an employee, investor, or entrepreneur, you naturally have real-world experience when it comes to marketplaces, industries, and key players that you've dealt with in the past. Even as a consumer, you have a sense of different solutions out there that cater to problems you directly experience.

In investing terms, this gives you a competitive advantage over others in the marketplace because you have access to knowledge that they don't have. Because of your direct experience in an industry, you could **KNOW** without a shadow of a doubt that a particular solution in sorely needed.

This informational advantage is what can lead to making good investment decisions that others fail to capitalize on. When you understand the fundamentals of the company and the marketplace, it brings a certain degree of certainty to the investment and mitigates the risk.

The inverse is also true. When you don't have a lot of information or knowledge about a particular marketplace, product, or solution, then you have a disadvantage as an investor. You have to quickly do your own research to figure out whether or not this is actually a good investment.

More often than not, you will be more easily swayed by the information the startup is providing you, leading to bad decisions that are based off of biased data. With less knowledge, you will be more easily swayed into making bad decisions, in the same way that consumers with little knowledge tend to overpay for products and services.

By investing in startups you understand, you'll avoid making some costly mistakes and poor decisions.

Tune Out Your Emotions (Or This Will Happen)

The surest path to making a bad decision is to simply follow your emotions.

Don't get me wrong. Sometimes, you can make very good decisions by listening to your emotions. However, when it comes to business, it's a recipe for disaster.

Sales people know that making a customer feel strong emotions is the easiest way to get them to take action and either buy a product or invest in an opportunity.

If you only listen to your emotions when it comes to studying an equity crowdfunding offering, you will end up "feeling good" about a particular startup, but you'll probably end up losing your money.

There is a difference between an investment "feeling" like a good decision in the moment compared to being an objectively good decision in the long run. The more logic that you apply to your decision-making process, the better.

You really have to try to tune out your emotions to the best of your ability. Look at the data, numbers, and metrics that underlie this company. Don't be seduced by a fancy video, compelling story, or positive future prospects.

Owners Should Be Marketers

As an investor in an equity crowdfunding campaign, you shouldn't just sit back on your laurels and wait for the startup to appreciate in value. You have the opportunity to speed up that process.

If we take a look at other investment opportunities, like Bitcoin, we can quickly see how the marketing and promotion that goes on in the community actually increases the value of the underlying asset.

The people who got in early into Bitcoin were significantly rewarded the more that it was talked about. So, they were actually incentivized to talk about the currency and get more people interested in it.

As an owner in a new startup company, you could sit back and let the company do all the world, or you could also become an evangelist for the product and brand. By helping to spread awareness about the startup, you'll help it get more users, traction, and thus increase in value.

Don't just be an owner of the startup. Also, be a marketer. The more you talk about the startup, the more people will also become interested in future funding rounds.

Expect To Lose Your Money (or Hit it Big)

I think it goes without saying but investing in ANY startup company is very risky. The majority of startup investments do not result in a positive ROI (even for seasoned investors).

A lot of startups will tank, go nowhere, or run out of funding before they are able to fully monetize their opportunity. Your risk of losing your investment is pretty obvious. The Ubers and DropBoxes are few and far in-between.

That being said, you also stand a lot to gain if you invest in the right team and the right startup. Even early employees in companies like Facebook grew their net worth into the tens if not hundreds of millions of dollars.

The reason why there is such a big opportunity is because of the way that startups can scale quickly using technology. When a startup gets product-market fit and has the right resources, it can easily blow up into a big company.

As an investor, you'll own a small piece of the pie, but it will be a gigantic pie. This is why your investment can appreciate a lot over time and well exceed the value of your entire portfolio. In fact, most VCs will only experience one major "home run" in their portfolio, which is what leads to most of the ROI of the fund.

Don't be Dumb. Do Your Homework

Don't rely on the due diligence of a crowdfunding platform. Just because they vet startups to some degree does not mean that every investment will be profitable.

The same goes for actual the startups. A startup will do everything in its power to convince you that they are a growing company with a bright future (because they want your investment). This means that the materials and data they provide you can be very biased.

It's important to do your own research and analysis for your investments. Verify the sources of the data that the startup brings up. Look into the industry yourself. Take a look at other existing solutions that are out there. If nothing else, plug the name of the company and the founders into Google to see what comes up.

Sometimes, as investors, we get so excited about a company and just simply *want* it to work out well. Unfortunately, the market doesn't care about our feelings. Logical analysis is the name of the game. Otherwise, you're going to lose your shirt.

Chapter 8: Industry Resources, Experts, and Service Providers

In the last few chapters, we covered the equity crowdfunding landscape and how you can raise money for your startup using an online fundraising platform. The next step is to assemble a team around your launch so that you can ensure its success. The right team can make or break your campaign.

I've assembled a list of some of the top resources, experts, and services providers in this industry that will help make the process of raising money much easier. This list will continue to expand and change over time as this new industry grows and develops. It's simply meant to help get you started.

Crowdfunding Experts and Service Providers

Mark Roderick: A corporate and securities lawyer who blogs about crowdfunding and fintech. He writes for portals and issuers.

CrowdfundX: An investor marketing agency that helps with media buying, investor targeting, and getting funding for Reg A+ offerings.

CrowdCheck: Due dilligence, disclosure, and compliance assistance. Sara Hanks, the CEO, is a corporate and securities attorney with over 30 years of experience.

Crowdfunding Lawyers: These guys handle Regulation A+, CF, D, and more.

Cutting Edge Capital: This company offers marketing services and help when it comes to doing a financial raise.

iDisclose: Legal technology platform designed to assist small businesses and startups with their legal needs.

Nathan Rose: The director of Assemble Advisory and an educator in this industry. He came on my podcast to discuss equity crowdfunding and how it works.

Salvador Briggman: I've been writing about equity crowdfunding since 2012 and YouTube channel where I talk about the subject.

Fundraising Tools and Resources

Aweber: A email list software tool that will let you send out emails, gauge response rates, and even set up automation series.

Buffer: Set up, schedule, and automate a social media account so that you don't have to worry about constantly posting updates.

Hunter: Get the emails of bloggers and journalists so that you can pitch them in the future.

Gmass: Send mass customized email messages to contacts or subscribers. Set follow-up messages also.

YouTube Live Stream: A free way to conduct a live webinar to answer questions, present a pitch, and persuade viewers to become investors.

Zoom: A premium tool to conduct live meetings and presentations. You can use this to discuss topics with investors.

Adexpresso: Great software tool for making it easier and less confusing to do Facebook ads.

Inspectlet: You can use this little tool to track your visitors on your website. See what they're looking at and how they are responding to your content.

Startup Stash: A directory of tools and resources to help you build your startup company

CoFoundersLab Templates: You'll find pitch decks, cold emails, NDAS, and other resources

<u>FoundersSuite:</u> A tool that will help you manage your pipeline of potential investors using a CRM.

<u>Product Hunt:</u> Marketplace to discover new tools, and also share your startup's product.

<u>Venture360:</u> Manage your deal pipeline from funding stages to custom permissions.

This industry is always evolving and changing. If I left you out of this list, shoot me an email and I can consider adding you to it. I hope this list of resources will help get you started as you're preparing for your equity crowdfunding campaign. There's a lot that goes into a raise, and I know it can be daunting, but it's my job to make that process much more manageable.

As you've gone through this book, you've gotten a crash course in equity crowdfunding, marketing, and startup fundraising. Now, it's time to act on that knowledge! Don't wait to get started. The sooner that you begin assembling your campaign, the better. Thorough preparation is the mother of success.

Chapter 9: Conclusion

There is a reason that the majority of new businesses fail in the first 1-5 years. There is a reason that most creative types aren't able to earn a living doing the type of work they love.

You might hate me for saying this, but I'm going to, because it's true. With crowdfunding, business, or life, you have to be willing to put in the work if you expect to reap the rewards.

You've already taken a major step. You've read through some of the proven techniques and strategies in this guide. Now, you have to actually take action. You have to execute on your plan!

I have never spoken with an entrepreneur who regrets having put himself or herself out there, for all of the world to discover. Yeah, it might be hard at first, but almost every person I've spoken with actually wishes they did it sooner. Even if they failed the first time, they regret not having tried it earlier.

When I look back at my early blog posts, podcasts, or YouTube videos, I cringe. They are sooo bad. But, by trying things out, I quickly learned what worked, and what didn't. I figured out how to improve, and now, I've gained a whole new set of skills. I'm much more confident in my own abilities and I'm excited about a bright future that's filled with possibilities.

Thank you for spending a bit of time with me learning the ins and outs of equity crowdfunding and marketing. I consider it a privilege to be able to pass on some of my knowledge.

You can get access to a FREE video on equity crowdfunding regulations here: http://www.crowdcrux.com/equitybonus

Happy Crowdfunding!

Salvador Briggman

"I learned many great lessons from my father, not the least of which was that you can fail at what you don't want, so you might as well take a chance on doing what you love." - Jim Carrey

About the Author

Salvador Briggman founded the popular blog, CrowdCrux, which has been cited by the New York Times, The Wallstreet Journal, CNN, and more. He helps entrepreneurs raise money on crowdfunding platforms like Kickstarter and Indiegogo. Last year, he helped nearly 400,000 individuals raise money from the crowd through his website, products, newsletter, and forum.

Made in United States
Orlando, FL
13 April 2022

16705348R00075